Firewall Knowledge
Complete Self-Assessment Guide

Table of Contents

About The Art of Service

The Art of Service, Business Process Architects since 2000, is dedicated to helping stakeholders achieve excellence.

Defining, designing, creating, and implementing a process to solve a stakeholders challenge or meet an objective is the most valuable role… In EVERY group, company, organization and department.

Unless you're talking a one-time, single-use project, there should be a process. Whether that process is managed and implemented by humans, AI, or a combination of the two, it needs to be designed by someone with a complex enough perspective to ask the right questions.

Someone capable of asking the right questions and step back and say, 'What are we really trying to accomplish here? And is there a different way to look at it?'

With The Art of Service's Standard Requirements Self-Assessments, we empower people who can do just that — whether their title is marketer, entrepreneur, manager, salesperson, consultant, Business Process Manager, executive assistant, IT Manager, CIO etc... —they are the people who rule the future. They are people who watch the process as it happens, and ask the right questions to make the process work better.

Contact us when you need any support with this Self-Assessment and any help with templates, blue-prints and examples of standard documents you might need:

http://theartofservice.com
service@theartofservice.com

Acknowledgments

This checklist was developed under the auspices of The Art of Service, chaired by Gerardus Blokdyk.

Representatives from several client companies participated in the preparation of this Self-Assessment.

In addition, we are thankful for the design and printing services provided.

Included Resources - how to access

Included with your purchase of the book is the Firewall Knowledge Self-Assessment Spreadsheet Dashboard which contains all questions and Self-Assessment areas and auto-generates insights, graphs, and project RACI planning - all with examples to get you started right away.

How? Simply send an email to
access@theartofservice.com
with this books' title in the subject to get the Firewall Knowledge Self Assessment Tool right away.

You will receive the following contents with New and Updated specific criteria:

- The latest quick edition of the book in PDF

- The latest complete edition of the book in PDF, which criteria correspond to the criteria in...

- The Self-Assessment Excel Dashboard, and...

- Example pre-filled Self-Assessment Excel Dashboard to get familiar with results generation

- In-depth specific Checklists covering the topic

- Project management checklists and templates to assist with implementation

INCLUDES LIFETIME SELF ASSESSMENT UPDATES

Every self assessment comes with Lifetime Updates and Lifetime Free Updated Books. Lifetime Updates is an industry-first feature which allows you to receive verified self assessment updates, ensuring you always have the most accurate information at your fingertips.

Get it now- you will be glad you did - do it now, before you forget.

Send an email to **access@theartofservice.com** with this books' title in the subject to get the Firewall Knowledge Self Assessment Tool right away.

Your feedback is invaluable to us

If you recently bought this book, we would love to hear from you! You can do this by writing a review on amazon (or the online store where you purchased this book) about your last purchase! As part of our continual service improvement process, we love to hear real client experiences and feedback.

How does it work?
To post a review on Amazon, just log in to your account and click on the Create Your Own Review button (under Customer Reviews) of the relevant product page. You can find examples of product reviews in Amazon. If you purchased from another online store, simply follow their procedures.

What happens when I submit my review?
Once you have submitted your review, send us an email at review@theartofservice.com with the link to your review so we can properly thank you for your feedback.

Purpose of this Self-Assessment

This Self-Assessment has been developed to improve understanding of the requirements and elements of Firewall Knowledge, based on best practices and standards in business process architecture, design and quality management.

It is designed to allow for a rapid Self-Assessment to determine how closely existing management practices and procedures correspond to the elements of the Self-Assessment.

The criteria of requirements and elements of Firewall Knowledge have been rephrased in the format of a Self-Assessment questionnaire, with a seven-criterion scoring system, as explained in this document.

In this format, even with limited background knowledge of

Firewall Knowledge, a manager can quickly review existing operations to determine how they measure up to the standards. This in turn can serve as the starting point of a 'gap analysis' to identify management tools or system elements that might usefully be implemented in the organization to help improve overall performance.

How to use the Self-Assessment

On the following pages are a series of questions to identify to what extent your Firewall Knowledge initiative is complete in comparison to the requirements set in standards.

To facilitate answering the questions, there is a space in front of each question to enter a score on a scale of '1' to '5'.

1 Strongly Disagree

2 Disagree

3 Neutral

4 Agree

5 Strongly Agree

Read the question and rate it with the following in front of mind:

'In my belief,
the answer to this question is clearly defined'.

There are two ways in which you can choose to interpret this statement;
1. how aware are you that the answer to the question is clearly defined
2. for more in-depth analysis you can choose to gather

evidence and confirm the answer to the question. This obviously will take more time, most Self-Assessment users opt for the first way to interpret the question and dig deeper later on based on the outcome of the overall Self-Assessment.

A score of '1' would mean that the answer is not clear at all, where a '5' would mean the answer is crystal clear and defined. Leave emtpy when the question is not applicable or you don't want to answer it, you can skip it without affecting your score. Write your score in the space provided.

After you have responded to all the appropriate statements in each section, compute your average score for that section, using the formula provided, and round to the nearest tenth. Then transfer to the corresponding spoke in the Firewall Knowledge Scorecard on the second next page of the Self-Assessment.

Your completed Firewall Knowledge Scorecard will give you a clear presentation of which Firewall Knowledge areas need attention.

Firewall Knowledge Scorecard Example

Example of how the finalized Scorecard can look like:

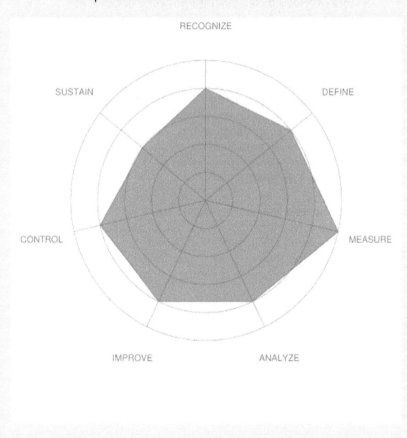

Firewall Knowledge Scorecard

Your Scores:

BEGINNING OF THE SELF-ASSESSMENT:

CRITERION #1: RECOGNIZE

INTENT: Be aware of the need for change. Recognize that there is an unfavorable variation, problem or symptom.

In my belief, the answer to this question is clearly defined:

5 Strongly Agree

4 Agree

3 Neutral

2 Disagree

1 Strongly Disagree

1. Who had the original idea?
<--- Score

2. How do you assess your Firewall Knowledge workforce capability and capacity needs, including skills, competencies, and staffing levels?
<--- Score

3. Are employees recognized or rewarded for

performance that demonstrates the highest levels of integrity?
<--- Score

4. What is the smallest subset of the problem you can usefully solve?
<--- Score

5. Who needs to know about Firewall Knowledge?
<--- Score

6. What prevents you from making the changes you know will make you a more effective Firewall Knowledge leader?
<--- Score

7. What are the minority interests and what amount of minority interests can be recognized?
<--- Score

8. What are the business objectives to be achieved with Firewall Knowledge?
<--- Score

9. What are the expected benefits of Firewall Knowledge to the business?
<--- Score

10. What does Firewall Knowledge success mean to the stakeholders?
<--- Score

11. What information do users need?
<--- Score

12. Should you invest in industry-recognized

qualications?
<--- Score

13. Looking at each person individually – does every one have the qualities which are needed to work in this group?
<--- Score

14. Do you have/need 24-hour access to key personnel?
<--- Score

15. When a Firewall Knowledge manager recognizes a problem, what options are available?
<--- Score

16. For your Firewall Knowledge project, identify and describe the business environment, is there more than one layer to the business environment?
<--- Score

17. Does Firewall Knowledge create potential expectations in other areas that need to be recognized and considered?
<--- Score

18. What else needs to be measured?
<--- Score

19. What are the timeframes required to resolve each of the issues/problems?
<--- Score

20. Have you identified your Firewall Knowledge key performance indicators?
<--- Score

21. Who defines the rules in relation to any given issue?
<--- Score

22. Do you know what you need to know about Firewall Knowledge?
<--- Score

23. Are problem definition and motivation clearly presented?
<--- Score

24. Who else hopes to benefit from it?
<--- Score

25. Will Firewall Knowledge deliverables need to be tested and, if so, by whom?
<--- Score

26. What is the problem or issue?
<--- Score

27. What do you need to start doing?
<--- Score

28. As a sponsor, customer or management, how important is it to meet goals, objectives?
<--- Score

29. To what extent does each concerned units management team recognize Firewall Knowledge as an effective investment?
<--- Score

30. How do you take a forward-looking perspective

in identifying Firewall Knowledge research related to market response and models?
<--- Score

31. What are your needs in relation to Firewall Knowledge skills, labor, equipment, and markets?
<--- Score

32. How are the Firewall Knowledge's objectives aligned to the organization's overall business strategy?
<--- Score

33. How can auditing be a preventative security measure?
<--- Score

34. How much are sponsors, customers, partners, stakeholders involved in Firewall Knowledge? In other words, what are the risks, if Firewall Knowledge does not deliver successfully?
<--- Score

35. What vendors make products that address the Firewall Knowledge needs?
<--- Score

36. Is it clear when you think of the day ahead of you what activities and tasks you need to complete?
<--- Score

37. What would happen if Firewall Knowledge weren't done?
<--- Score

38. Consider your own Firewall Knowledge project,

what types of organizational problems do you think might be causing or affecting your problem, based on the work done so far?
<--- Score

39. Think about the people you identified for your Firewall Knowledge project and the project responsibilities you would assign to them. what kind of training do you think they would need to perform these responsibilities effectively?
<--- Score

40. Are your goals realistic? Do you need to redefine your problem? Perhaps the problem has changed or maybe you have reached your goal and need to set a new one?
<--- Score

41. What should be considered when identifying available resources, constraints, and deadlines?
<--- Score

42. Is the need for organizational change recognized?
<--- Score

43. Are there any specific expectations or concerns about the Firewall Knowledge team, Firewall Knowledge itself?
<--- Score

44. Do you need different information or graphics?
<--- Score

45. What needs to be done?
<--- Score

46. Are there Firewall Knowledge problems defined?
<--- Score

47. How are you going to measure success?
<--- Score

48. How does it fit into your organizational needs and tasks?
<--- Score

49. What tools and technologies are needed for a custom Firewall Knowledge project?
<--- Score

50. Are there recognized Firewall Knowledge problems?
<--- Score

51. What situation(s) led to this Firewall Knowledge Self Assessment?
<--- Score

52. Will new equipment/products be required to facilitate Firewall Knowledge delivery, for example is new software needed?
<--- Score

53. Do you need to avoid or amend any Firewall Knowledge activities?
<--- Score

54. What problems are you facing and how do you consider Firewall Knowledge will circumvent those obstacles?
<--- Score

55. What activities does the governance board need to consider?
<--- Score

Add up total points for this section:
_ _ _ _ _ = Total points for this section

Divided by: _ _ _ _ _ _ (number of statements answered) = _ _ _ _ _ _
Average score for this section

Transfer your score to the Firewall Knowledge Index at the beginning of the Self-Assessment.

CRITERION #2: DEFINE:

INTENT: Formulate the business problem. Define the problem, needs and objectives.

In my belief, the answer to this question is clearly defined:

5 Strongly Agree

4 Agree

3 Neutral

2 Disagree

1 Strongly Disagree

1. What defines best in class?
<--- Score

2. What would be the goal or target for a Firewall Knowledge's improvement team?
<--- Score

3. What scope do you want your strategy to cover?
<--- Score

4. How is the team tracking and documenting its work?
<--- Score

5. What happens if Firewall Knowledge's scope changes?
<--- Score

6. Are improvement team members fully trained on Firewall Knowledge?
<--- Score

7. Is Firewall Knowledge linked to key business goals and objectives?
<--- Score

8. What are the rough order estimates on cost savings/ opportunities that Firewall Knowledge brings?
<--- Score

9. What is the definition of success?
<--- Score

10. Is there a critical path to deliver Firewall Knowledge results?
<--- Score

11. Is data collected and displayed to better understand customer(s) critical needs and requirements.
<--- Score

12. What constraints exist that might impact the team?
<--- Score

13. Are team charters developed?
<--- Score

14. Are there any constraints known that bear on the ability to perform Firewall Knowledge work? How is the team addressing them?
<--- Score

15. What is in scope?
<--- Score

16. Are there different segments of customers?
<--- Score

17. Has a high-level 'as is' process map been completed, verified and validated?
<--- Score

18. Are customer(s) identified and segmented according to their different needs and requirements?
<--- Score

19. Is there a completed, verified, and validated high-level 'as is' (not 'should be' or 'could be') business process map?
<--- Score

20. Do you all define Firewall Knowledge in the same way?
<--- Score

21. What is the context?
<--- Score

22. What specifically is the problem? Where does it

occur? When does it occur? What is its extent?
<--- Score

23. Is the team formed and are team leaders (Coaches and Management Leads) assigned?
<--- Score

24. How does the Firewall Knowledge manager ensure against scope creep?
<--- Score

25. Is a fully trained team formed, supported, and committed to work on the Firewall Knowledge improvements?
<--- Score

26. Is the team equipped with available and reliable resources?
<--- Score

27. Is the improvement team aware of the different versions of a process: what they think it is vs. what it actually is vs. what it should be vs. what it could be?
<--- Score

28. How do you keep key subject matter experts in the loop?
<--- Score

29. How will variation in the actual durations of each activity be dealt with to ensure that the expected Firewall Knowledge results are met?
<--- Score

30. What critical content must be communicated – who, what, when, where, and how?

<--- Score

31. How do you think the partners involved in Firewall Knowledge would have defined success?
<--- Score

32. Is it clearly defined in and to your organization what you do?
<--- Score

33. How was the 'as is' process map developed, reviewed, verified and validated?
<--- Score

34. Are resources adequate for the scope?
<--- Score

35. Is there regularly 100% attendance at the team meetings? If not, have appointed substitutes attended to preserve cross-functionality and full representation?
<--- Score

36. Do the problem and goal statements meet the SMART criteria (specific, measurable, attainable, relevant, and time-bound)?
<--- Score

37. Does the team have regular meetings?
<--- Score

38. What is out of scope?
<--- Score

39. Is there a completed SIPOC representation, describing the Suppliers, Inputs, Process, Outputs, and

Customers?
<--- Score

40. How and when will the baselines be defined?
<--- Score

41. What are the dynamics of the communication plan?
<--- Score

42. How often are the team meetings?
<--- Score

43. Is Firewall Knowledge currently on schedule according to the plan?
<--- Score

44. What is in the scope and what is not in scope?
<--- Score

45. How will the Firewall Knowledge team and the organization measure complete success of Firewall Knowledge?
<--- Score

46. How can the value of Firewall Knowledge be defined?
<--- Score

47. Does the scope remain the same?
<--- Score

48. Has a project plan, Gantt chart, or similar been developed/completed?
<--- Score

49. Have all basic functions of Firewall Knowledge been defined?
<--- Score

50. In what way can you redefine the criteria of choice clients have in your category in your favor?
<--- Score

51. What are the record-keeping requirements of Firewall Knowledge activities?
<--- Score

52. Is the team adequately staffed with the desired cross-functionality? If not, what additional resources are available to the team?
<--- Score

53. What are the boundaries of the scope? What is in bounds and what is not? What is the start point? What is the stop point?
<--- Score

54. Has anyone else (internal or external to the organization) attempted to solve this problem or a similar one before? If so, what knowledge can be leveraged from these previous efforts?
<--- Score

55. Are customers identified and high impact areas defined?
<--- Score

56. Have the customer needs been translated into specific, measurable requirements? How?
<--- Score

57. Is the Firewall Knowledge scope manageable?
<--- Score

58. Who are the Firewall Knowledge improvement team members, including Management Leads and Coaches?
<--- Score

59. You may have created your quality measures at a time when you lacked resources, technology wasn't up to the required standard, or low service levels were the industry norm. Have those circumstances changed?
<--- Score

60. Are required metrics defined, what are they?
<--- Score

61. Are accountability and ownership for Firewall Knowledge clearly defined?
<--- Score

62. Have specific policy objectives been defined?
<--- Score

63. Are approval levels defined for contracts and supplements to contracts?
<--- Score

64. Has the improvement team collected the 'voice of the customer' (obtained feedback – qualitative and quantitative)?
<--- Score

65. Are business processes mapped?
<--- Score

66. Has/have the customer(s) been identified?
<--- Score

67. Has the Firewall Knowledge work been fairly and/ or equitably divided and delegated among team members who are qualified and capable to perform the work? Has everyone contributed?
<--- Score

68. Is the current 'as is' process being followed? If not, what are the discrepancies?
<--- Score

69. Is the scope of Firewall Knowledge defined?
<--- Score

70. Will team members regularly document their Firewall Knowledge work?
<--- Score

71. What customer feedback methods were used to solicit their input?
<--- Score

72. How do you hand over Firewall Knowledge context?
<--- Score

73. Has a team charter been developed and communicated?
<--- Score

74. When is the estimated completion date?
<--- Score

75. If substitutes have been appointed, have they been briefed on the Firewall Knowledge goals and received regular communications as to the progress to date?
<--- Score

76. Scope of sensitive information?
<--- Score

77. Are different versions of process maps needed to account for the different types of inputs?
<--- Score

78. How would you define Firewall Knowledge leadership?
<--- Score

79. Has everyone on the team, including the team leaders, been properly trained?
<--- Score

80. When was the Firewall Knowledge start date?
<--- Score

81. How would you define the culture at your organization, how susceptible is it to Firewall Knowledge changes?
<--- Score

82. What are the tasks and definitions?
<--- Score

83. What is the scope of the Firewall Knowledge effort?
<--- Score

84. What was the context?
<--- Score

85. Has the direction changed at all during the course of Firewall Knowledge? If so, when did it change and why?
<--- Score

86. Is the Firewall Knowledge scope complete and appropriately sized?
<--- Score

87. What is the scope of Firewall Knowledge?
<--- Score

88. What baselines are required to be defined and managed?
<--- Score

89. How did the Firewall Knowledge manager receive input to the development of a Firewall Knowledge improvement plan and the estimated completion dates/times of each activity?
<--- Score

90. What key business process output measure(s) does Firewall Knowledge leverage and how?
<--- Score

91. When are meeting minutes sent out? Who is on the distribution list?
<--- Score

92. What are the Roles and Responsibilities for each team member and its leadership? Where is this documented?

<--- Score

93. Have all of the relationships been defined properly?
<--- Score

94. Are roles and responsibilities formally defined?
<--- Score

95. Who defines (or who defined) the rules and roles?
<--- Score

96. Will team members perform Firewall Knowledge work when assigned and in a timely fashion?
<--- Score

97. Is full participation by members in regularly held team meetings guaranteed?
<--- Score

98. Is Firewall Knowledge required?
<--- Score

99. What are the compelling business reasons for embarking on Firewall Knowledge?
<--- Score

100. How do you gather Firewall Knowledge requirements?
<--- Score

101. Is there a Firewall Knowledge management charter, including business case, problem and goal statements, scope, milestones, roles and responsibilities, communication plan?
<--- Score

102. Is the team sponsored by a champion or business leader?
<--- Score

Add up total points for this section:
_ _ _ _ _ = Total points for this section

Divided by: _ _ _ _ _ _ (number of
statements answered) = _ _ _ _ _ _
Average score for this section

Transfer your score to the Firewall
Knowledge Index at the beginning of
the Self-Assessment.

CRITERION #3: MEASURE:

INTENT: Gather the correct data. Measure the current performance and evolution of the situation.

In my belief, the answer to this question is clearly defined:

5 Strongly Agree

4 Agree

3 Neutral

2 Disagree

1 Strongly Disagree

1. How do you measure lifecycle phases?
<--- Score

2. Which measures and indicators matter?
<--- Score

3. How do you measure success?
<--- Score

4. What are the agreed upon definitions of the high impact areas, defect(s), unit(s), and opportunities that will figure into the process capability metrics?
<--- Score

5. Have changes been properly/adequately analyzed for effect?
<--- Score

6. Is data collection planned and executed?
<--- Score

7. How do your measurements capture actionable Firewall Knowledge information for use in exceeding your customers expectations and securing your customers engagement?
<--- Score

8. Does the Firewall Knowledge task fit the client's priorities?
<--- Score

9. What are the types and number of measures to use?
<--- Score

10. How large is the gap between current performance and the customer-specified (goal) performance?
<--- Score

11. What would be a real cause for concern?
<--- Score

12. What charts has the team used to display the components of variation in the process?
<--- Score

13. Are there any easy-to-implement alternatives to Firewall Knowledge? Sometimes other solutions are available that do not require the cost implications of a full-blown project?
<--- Score

14. What potential environmental factors impact the Firewall Knowledge effort?
<--- Score

15. Why do the measurements/indicators matter?
<--- Score

16. What is the right balance of time and resources between investigation, analysis, and discussion and dissemination?
<--- Score

17. Are high impact defects defined and identified in the business process?
<--- Score

18. What methods are feasible and acceptable to estimate the impact of reforms?
<--- Score

19. What disadvantage does this cause for the user?
<--- Score

20. Does your organization systematically track and analyze outcomes related for accountability and quality improvement?
<--- Score

21. How do you identify and analyze stakeholders and

their interests?

<--- Score

22. Have the concerns of stakeholders to help identify and define potential barriers been obtained and analyzed?

<--- Score

23. Are losses documented, analyzed, and remedial processes developed to prevent future losses?

<--- Score

24. What has the team done to assure the stability and accuracy of the measurement process?

<--- Score

25. Are the units of measure consistent?

<--- Score

26. What are your key Firewall Knowledge organizational performance measures, including key short and longer-term financial measures?

<--- Score

27. How to cause the change?

<--- Score

28. What are the costs of reform?

<--- Score

29. Are you aware of what could cause a problem?

<--- Score

30. Are process variation components displayed/ communicated using suitable charts, graphs, plots?

<--- Score

31. Was a data collection plan established?
<--- Score

32. What particular quality tools did the team find helpful in establishing measurements?
<--- Score

33. What key measures identified indicate the performance of the business process?
<--- Score

34. How will success or failure be measured?
<--- Score

35. How will you measure success?
<--- Score

36. How do you aggregate measures across priorities?
<--- Score

37. What are the key input variables? What are the key process variables? What are the key output variables?
<--- Score

38. How is performance measured?
<--- Score

39. How are measurements made?
<--- Score

40. Who should receive measurement reports?
<--- Score

41. What causes mismanagement?
<--- Score

42. When is Root Cause Analysis Required?

<--- Score

43. How do you do risk analysis of rare, cascading, catastrophic events?

<--- Score

44. Are key measures identified and agreed upon?

<--- Score

45. What are your customers expectations and measures?

<--- Score

46. What data was collected (past, present, future/ ongoing)?

<--- Score

47. Do you aggressively reward and promote the people who have the biggest impact on creating excellent Firewall Knowledge services/products?

<--- Score

48. Does Firewall Knowledge analysis show the relationships among important Firewall Knowledge factors?

<--- Score

49. How do you measure efficient delivery of Firewall Knowledge services?

<--- Score

50. Have you found any 'ground fruit' or 'low-hanging fruit' for immediate remedies to the gap in performance?

<--- Score

51. What measurements are being captured?
<--- Score

52. What evidence is there and what is measured?
<--- Score

53. What is the total cost related to deploying Firewall Knowledge, including any consulting or professional services?
<--- Score

54. How is the value delivered by Firewall Knowledge being measured?
<--- Score

55. How do you control the overall costs of your work processes?
<--- Score

56. Does Firewall Knowledge analysis isolate the fundamental causes of problems?
<--- Score

57. What measurements are possible, practicable and meaningful?
<--- Score

58. Among the Firewall Knowledge product and service cost to be estimated, which is considered hardest to estimate?
<--- Score

59. Does Firewall Knowledge systematically track and analyze outcomes for accountability and quality

improvement?
<--- Score

60. Is Process Variation Displayed/Communicated?
<--- Score

61. What do you measure and why?
<--- Score

62. Have you made assumptions about the shape of the future, particularly its impact on your customers and competitors?
<--- Score

63. Are the measurements objective?
<--- Score

64. What causes investor action?
<--- Score

65. Is long term and short term variability accounted for?
<--- Score

66. How will you measure your Firewall Knowledge effectiveness?
<--- Score

67. What are your key Firewall Knowledge indicators that you will measure, analyze and track?
<--- Score

68. How will measures be used to manage and adapt?
<--- Score

69. Will Firewall Knowledge have an impact on current

business continuity, disaster recovery processes and/ or infrastructure?

<--- Score

70. How can you measure the performance?

<--- Score

71. What is an unallowable cost?

<--- Score

72. Is the solution cost-effective?

<--- Score

73. Where is it measured?

<--- Score

74. Is there a Performance Baseline?

<--- Score

75. What relevant entities could be measured?

<--- Score

76. Did you tackle the cause or the symptom?

<--- Score

77. Is key measure data collection planned and executed, process variation displayed and communicated and performance baselined?

<--- Score

78. What causes extra work or rework?

<--- Score

79. Who participated in the data collection for measurements?

<--- Score

80. What could cause you to change course?
<--- Score

81. What could cause delays in the schedule?
<--- Score

82. Are you taking your company in the direction of better and revenue or cheaper and cost?
<--- Score

83. How will your organization measure success?
<--- Score

84. How is progress measured?
<--- Score

85. Are missed Firewall Knowledge opportunities costing your organization money?
<--- Score

86. What causes innovation to fail or succeed in your organization?
<--- Score

87. Can you measure the return on analysis?
<--- Score

88. Is a solid data collection plan established that includes measurement systems analysis?
<--- Score

89. Is it possible to estimate the impact of unanticipated complexity such as wrong or failed assumptions, feedback, etc. on proposed reforms?
<--- Score

90. Do staff have the necessary skills to collect, analyze, and report data?
<--- Score

91. Is data collected on key measures that were identified?
<--- Score

92. Can you do Firewall Knowledge without complex (expensive) analysis?
<--- Score

Add up total points for this section:
_ _ _ _ _ = Total points for this section

Divided by: _ _ _ _ _ _ (number of statements answered) = _ _ _ _ _ _
Average score for this section

Transfer your score to the Firewall Knowledge Index at the beginning of the Self-Assessment.

CRITERION #4: ANALYZE:

INTENT: Analyze causes, assumptions
and hypotheses.

In my belief, the answer to this
question is clearly defined:

5 Strongly Agree

4 Agree

3 Neutral

2 Disagree

1 Strongly Disagree

1. Can you add value to the current Firewall
Knowledge decision-making process (largely
qualitative) by incorporating uncertainty modeling
(more quantitative)?
<--- Score

2. What is your organizations process which leads to
recognition of value generation?
<--- Score

3. How is the way you as the leader think and process information affecting your organizational culture?
<--- Score

4. Think about the functions involved in your Firewall Knowledge project, what processes flow from these functions?
<--- Score

5. How does the organization define, manage, and improve its Firewall Knowledge processes?
<--- Score

6. An organizationally feasible system request is one that considers the mission, goals and objectives of the organization. Key questions are: is the Firewall Knowledge solution request practical and will it solve a problem or take advantage of an opportunity to achieve company goals?
<--- Score

7. What are the best opportunities for value improvement?
<--- Score

8. What tools were used to generate the list of possible causes?
<--- Score

9. Is the gap/opportunity displayed and communicated in financial terms?
<--- Score

10. What conclusions were drawn from the team's data collection and analysis? How did the team reach these conclusions?

<--- Score

11. What were the financial benefits resulting from any 'ground fruit or low-hanging fruit' (quick fixes)?
<--- Score

12. Did any additional data need to be collected?
<--- Score

13. Is the required Firewall Knowledge data gathered?
<--- Score

14. How often will data be collected for measures?
<--- Score

15. Were Pareto charts (or similar) used to portray the 'heavy hitters' (or key sources of variation)?
<--- Score

16. How is Firewall Knowledge data gathered?
<--- Score

17. A compounding model resolution with available relevant data can often provide insight towards a solution methodology; which Firewall Knowledge models, tools and techniques are necessary?
<--- Score

18. Were there any improvement opportunities identified from the process analysis?
<--- Score

19. What did the team gain from developing a sub-process map?
<--- Score

20. How do you identify specific Firewall Knowledge investment opportunities and emerging trends?
<--- Score

21. What tools were used to narrow the list of possible causes?
<--- Score

22. Have any additional benefits been identified that will result from closing all or most of the gaps?
<--- Score

23. What quality tools were used to get through the analyze phase?
<--- Score

24. How do you implement and manage your work processes to ensure that they meet design requirements?
<--- Score

25. What other organizational variables, such as reward systems or communication systems, affect the performance of this Firewall Knowledge process?
<--- Score

26. Identify an operational issue in your organization. for example, could a particular task be done more quickly or more efficiently by Firewall Knowledge?
<--- Score

27. What are the revised rough estimates of the financial savings/opportunity for Firewall Knowledge improvements?
<--- Score

28. What process should you select for improvement?
<--- Score

29. When conducting a business process reengineering study, what do you look for when trying to identify business processes to change?
<--- Score

30. What are your best practices for minimizing Firewall Knowledge project risk, while demonstrating incremental value and quick wins throughout the Firewall Knowledge project lifecycle?
<--- Score

31. How was the detailed process map generated, verified, and validated?
<--- Score

32. Did any value-added analysis or 'lean thinking' take place to identify some of the gaps shown on the 'as is' process map?
<--- Score

33. What is the cost of poor quality as supported by the team's analysis?
<--- Score

34. How do mission and objectives affect the Firewall Knowledge processes of your organization?
<--- Score

35. What were the crucial 'moments of truth' on the process map?
<--- Score

36. Where is Firewall Knowledge data gathered?

<--- Score

37. Do several people in different organizational units assist with the Firewall Knowledge process?
<--- Score

38. What data is gathered?
<--- Score

39. Are Firewall Knowledge changes recognized early enough to be approved through the regular process?
<--- Score

40. Where is the data coming from to measure compliance?
<--- Score

41. What does the data say about the performance of the business process?
<--- Score

42. What are your Firewall Knowledge processes?
<--- Score

43. Was a detailed process map created to amplify critical steps of the 'as is' business process?
<--- Score

44. What are your key performance measures or indicators and in-process measures for the control and improvement of your Firewall Knowledge processes?
<--- Score

45. What are your current levels and trends in key measures or indicators of Firewall Knowledge product

and process performance that are important to and directly serve your customers? How do these results compare with the performance of your competitors and other organizations with similar offerings?
<--- Score

46. Do your contracts/agreements contain data security obligations?
<--- Score

47. What controls do you have in place to protect data?
<--- Score

48. Do your employees have the opportunity to do what they do best everyday?
<--- Score

49. Is the performance gap determined?
<--- Score

50. Were any designed experiments used to generate additional insight into the data analysis?
<--- Score

51. Is Data and process analysis, root cause analysis and quantifying the gap/opportunity in place?
<--- Score

52. How do you promote understanding that opportunity for improvement is not criticism of the status quo, or the people who created the status quo?
<--- Score

53. Do you, as a leader, bounce back quickly from setbacks?

<--- Score

54. Was a cause-and-effect diagram used to explore the different types of causes (or sources of variation)?
<--- Score

55. Do your leaders quickly bounce back from setbacks?
<--- Score

56. How do your work systems and key work processes relate to and capitalize on your core competencies?
<--- Score

57. Have the problem and goal statements been updated to reflect the additional knowledge gained from the analyze phase?
<--- Score

58. Are gaps between current performance and the goal performance identified?
<--- Score

59. What are your current levels and trends in key Firewall Knowledge measures or indicators of product and process performance that are important to and directly serve your customers?
<--- Score

60. What Firewall Knowledge data do you gather or use now?
<--- Score

61. Is the suppliers process defined and controlled?
<--- Score

62. Is the Firewall Knowledge process severely broken such that a re-design is necessary?
<--- Score

63. How do you measure the operational performance of your key work systems and processes, including productivity, cycle time, and other appropriate measures of process effectiveness, efficiency, and innovation?
<--- Score

Add up total points for this section:
_ _ _ _ _ = Total points for this section

Divided by: _ _ _ _ _ _ (number of statements answered) = _ _ _ _ _ _
Average score for this section

Transfer your score to the Firewall Knowledge Index at the beginning of the Self-Assessment.

CRITERION #5: IMPROVE:

INTENT: Develop a practical solution. Innovate, establish and test the solution and to measure the results.

In my belief, the answer to this question is clearly defined:

5 Strongly Agree

4 Agree

3 Neutral

2 Disagree

1 Strongly Disagree

1. Is the scope clearly documented?
<--- Score

2. How do you measure progress and evaluate training effectiveness?
<--- Score

3. How does the solution remove the key sources of issues discovered in the analyze phase?

<--- Score

4. Who controls key decisions that will be made?
<--- Score

5. Is pilot data collected and analyzed?
<--- Score

6. How can you improve performance?
<--- Score

7. Why improve in the first place?
<--- Score

8. Is there a small-scale pilot for proposed improvement(s)? What conclusions were drawn from the outcomes of a pilot?
<--- Score

9. Risk factors: what are the characteristics of Firewall Knowledge that make it risky?
<--- Score

10. Can you identify any significant risks or exposures to Firewall Knowledge third- parties (vendors, service providers, alliance partners etc) that concern you?
<--- Score

11. Risk Identification: What are the possible risk events your organization faces in relation to Firewall Knowledge?
<--- Score

12. How can skill-level changes improve Firewall Knowledge?
<--- Score

13. What were the underlying assumptions on the cost-benefit analysis?
<--- Score

14. How do you measure improved Firewall Knowledge service perception, and satisfaction?
<--- Score

15. How will the team or the process owner(s) monitor the implementation plan to see that it is working as intended?
<--- Score

16. Will the controls trigger any other risks?
<--- Score

17. Explorations of the frontiers of Firewall Knowledge will help you build influence, improve Firewall Knowledge, optimize decision making, and sustain change, what is your approach?
<--- Score

18. Was a pilot designed for the proposed solution(s)?
<--- Score

19. How do you link measurement and risk?
<--- Score

20. Who will be using the results of the measurement activities?
<--- Score

21. How will you know that you have improved?
<--- Score

22. Who are the people involved in developing and implementing Firewall Knowledge?
<--- Score

23. Can the solution be designed and implemented within an acceptable time period?
<--- Score

24. Are there any constraints (technical, political, cultural, or otherwise) that would inhibit certain solutions?
<--- Score

25. How does the team improve its work?
<--- Score

26. For decision problems, how do you develop a decision statement?
<--- Score

27. Does the goal represent a desired result that can be measured?
<--- Score

28. What is the team's contingency plan for potential problems occurring in implementation?
<--- Score

29. Are risk triggers captured?
<--- Score

30. How do you manage and improve your Firewall Knowledge work systems to deliver customer value and achieve organizational success and sustainability?
<--- Score

31. What is the magnitude of the improvements?
<--- Score

32. What is Firewall Knowledge's impact on utilizing the best solution(s)?
<--- Score

33. In the past few months, what is the smallest change you have made that has had the biggest positive result? What was it about that small change that produced the large return?
<--- Score

34. What can you do to improve?
<--- Score

35. Do those selected for the Firewall Knowledge team have a good general understanding of what Firewall Knowledge is all about?
<--- Score

36. What improvements have been achieved?
<--- Score

37. Are improved process ('should be') maps modified based on pilot data and analysis?
<--- Score

38. What error proofing will be done to address some of the discrepancies observed in the 'as is' process?
<--- Score

39. How do you decide how much to remunerate an employee?
<--- Score

40. What to do with the results or outcomes of measurements?
<--- Score

41. What is the risk?
<--- Score

42. Is supporting Firewall Knowledge documentation required?
<--- Score

43. How will you know when its improved?
<--- Score

44. What lessons, if any, from a pilot were incorporated into the design of the full-scale solution?
<--- Score

45. To what extent does management recognize Firewall Knowledge as a tool to increase the results?
<--- Score

46. What tools were used to evaluate the potential solutions?
<--- Score

47. Is the implementation plan designed?
<--- Score

48. Is a solution implementation plan established, including schedule/work breakdown structure, resources, risk management plan, cost/budget, and control plan?
<--- Score

49. Is the solution technically practical?

<--- Score

50. What tools were most useful during the improve phase?
<--- Score

51. Were any criteria developed to assist the team in testing and evaluating potential solutions?
<--- Score

52. What attendant changes will need to be made to ensure that the solution is successful?
<--- Score

53. How do you improve productivity?
<--- Score

54. How do you stay flexible and focused to recognize larger Firewall Knowledge results?
<--- Score

55. Is the optimal solution selected based on testing and analysis?
<--- Score

56. What resources are required for the improvement efforts?
<--- Score

57. What does the 'should be' process map/design look like?
<--- Score

58. How did the team generate the list of possible solutions?
<--- Score

59. What needs improvement? Why?
<--- Score

60. Are possible solutions generated and tested?
<--- Score

61. Are you assessing Firewall Knowledge and risk?
<--- Score

62. How risky is your organization?
<--- Score

63. How will you know that a change is an improvement?
<--- Score

64. What tools do you use once you have decided on a Firewall Knowledge strategy and more importantly how do you choose?
<--- Score

65. How do you measure risk?
<--- Score

66. How will the organization know that the solution worked?
<--- Score

67. For estimation problems, how do you develop an estimation statement?
<--- Score

68. What communications are necessary to support the implementation of the solution?
<--- Score

69. Do you combine technical expertise with business knowledge and Firewall Knowledge Key topics include lifecycles, development approaches, requirements and how to make a business case?
<--- Score

70. What actually has to improve and by how much?
<--- Score

71. How do you improve your likelihood of success ?
<--- Score

72. What do you want to improve?
<--- Score

73. How do you improve Firewall Knowledge service perception, and satisfaction?
<--- Score

74. What are the implications of the one critical Firewall Knowledge decision 10 minutes, 10 months, and 10 years from now?
<--- Score

75. Are the best solutions selected?
<--- Score

76. Risk events: what are the things that could go wrong?
<--- Score

77. How do you go about comparing Firewall Knowledge approaches/solutions?
<--- Score

78. Is the measure of success for Firewall Knowledge understandable to a variety of people?
<--- Score

79. Who will be responsible for documenting the Firewall Knowledge requirements in detail?
<--- Score

80. How do you define the solutions' scope?
<--- Score

81. Is there a high likelihood that any recommendations will achieve their intended results?
<--- Score

82. Is there a cost/benefit analysis of optimal solution(s)?
<--- Score

83. Is a contingency plan established?
<--- Score

84. How will you measure the results?
<--- Score

85. Who controls the risk?
<--- Score

86. At what point will vulnerability assessments be performed once Firewall Knowledge is put into production (e.g., ongoing Risk Management after implementation)?
<--- Score

87. What is the implementation plan?
<--- Score

88. What tools were used to tap into the creativity and encourage 'outside the box' thinking?
<--- Score

89. How do you keep improving Firewall Knowledge?
<--- Score

90. Are new and improved process ('should be') maps developed?
<--- Score

91. What went well, what should change, what can improve?
<--- Score

92. How do the Firewall Knowledge results compare with the performance of your competitors and other organizations with similar offerings?
<--- Score

93. Describe the design of the pilot and what tests were conducted, if any?
<--- Score

Add up total points for this section:
_ _ _ _ _ = Total points for this section

Divided by: _ _ _ _ _ _ (number of statements answered) = _ _ _ _ _ _
Average score for this section

Transfer your score to the Firewall Knowledge Index at the beginning of the Self-Assessment.

CRITERION #6: CONTROL:

INTENT: Implement the practical solution. Maintain the performance and correct possible complications.

In my belief, the answer to this question is clearly defined:

5 Strongly Agree

4 Agree

3 Neutral

2 Disagree

1 Strongly Disagree

1. Are the planned controls working?
<--- Score

2. What are you attempting to measure/monitor?
<--- Score

3. Where do ideas that reach policy makers and planners as proposals for Firewall Knowledge strengthening and reform actually originate?

<--- Score

4. Has the improved process and its steps been standardized?
<--- Score

5. How can you best use all of your knowledge repositories to enhance learning and sharing?
<--- Score

6. Is a response plan in place for when the input, process, or output measures indicate an 'out-of-control' condition?
<--- Score

7. Is new knowledge gained imbedded in the response plan?
<--- Score

8. Are controls in place and consistently applied?
<--- Score

9. What is the best design framework for Firewall Knowledge organization now that, in a post industrial-age if the top-down, command and control model is no longer relevant?
<--- Score

10. Are documented procedures clear and easy to follow for the operators?
<--- Score

11. What should you measure to verify efficiency gains?
<--- Score

12. Are you measuring, monitoring and predicting Firewall Knowledge activities to optimize operations and profitability, and enhancing outcomes?
<--- Score

13. Does the response plan contain a definite closed loop continual improvement scheme (e.g., plan-do-check-act)?
<--- Score

14. How will the process owner and team be able to hold the gains?
<--- Score

15. What do you stand for--and what are you against?
<--- Score

16. Will any special training be provided for results interpretation?
<--- Score

17. Have new or revised work instructions resulted?
<--- Score

18. Is a response plan established and deployed?
<--- Score

19. Is there a Firewall Knowledge Communication plan covering who needs to get what information when?
<--- Score

20. What other areas of the organization might benefit from the Firewall Knowledge team's improvements, knowledge, and learning?
<--- Score

21. Does a troubleshooting guide exist or is it needed?
<--- Score

22. Are suggested corrective/restorative actions indicated on the response plan for known causes to problems that might surface?
<--- Score

23. What quality tools were useful in the control phase?
<--- Score

24. What adjustments to the strategies are needed?
<--- Score

25. Are there documented procedures?
<--- Score

26. Is there a standardized process?
<--- Score

27. Does Firewall Knowledge appropriately measure and monitor risk?
<--- Score

28. Who controls critical resources?
<--- Score

29. How will new or emerging customer needs/requirements be checked/communicated to orient the process toward meeting the new specifications and continually reducing variation?
<--- Score

30. What can you control?

<--- Score

31. Do the Firewall Knowledge decisions you make today help people and the planet tomorrow?
<--- Score

32. Is there documentation that will support the successful operation of the improvement?
<--- Score

33. What are the critical parameters to watch?
<--- Score

34. How do senior leaders actions reflect a commitment to the organizations Firewall Knowledge values?
<--- Score

35. How do you select, collect, align, and integrate Firewall Knowledge data and information for tracking daily operations and overall organizational performance, including progress relative to strategic objectives and action plans?
<--- Score

36. How will the process owner verify improvement in present and future sigma levels, process capabilities?
<--- Score

37. What are your results for key measures or indicators of the accomplishment of your Firewall Knowledge strategy and action plans, including building and strengthening core competencies?
<--- Score

38. Act/Adjust: What Do you Need to Do Differently?

<--- Score

39. Are the planned controls in place?
<--- Score

40. Will existing staff require re-training, for example, to learn new business processes?
<--- Score

41. Who will be in control?
<--- Score

42. How will report readings be checked to effectively monitor performance?
<--- Score

43. How is change control managed?
<--- Score

44. Are operating procedures consistent?
<--- Score

45. How will input, process, and output variables be checked to detect for sub-optimal conditions?
<--- Score

46. What are the key elements of your Firewall Knowledge performance improvement system, including your evaluation, organizational learning, and innovation processes?
<--- Score

47. What is the control/monitoring plan?
<--- Score

48. What is the recommended frequency of auditing?

<--- Score

49. How do you plan on providing proper recognition and disclosure of supporting companies?
<--- Score

50. Implementation Planning: is a pilot needed to test the changes before a full roll out occurs?
<--- Score

51. How do you establish and deploy modified action plans if circumstances require a shift in plans and rapid execution of new plans?
<--- Score

52. What should the next improvement project be that is related to Firewall Knowledge?
<--- Score

53. Will the team be available to assist members in planning investigations?
<--- Score

54. Does the Firewall Knowledge performance meet the customer's requirements?
<--- Score

55. Does job training on the documented procedures need to be part of the process team's education and training?
<--- Score

56. Is there a recommended audit plan for routine surveillance inspections of Firewall Knowledge's gains?
<--- Score

57. Against what alternative is success being measured?
<--- Score

58. How do controls support value?
<--- Score

59. How might the organization capture best practices and lessons learned so as to leverage improvements across the business?
<--- Score

60. Can support from partners be adjusted?
<--- Score

61. What do your reports reflect?
<--- Score

62. Is there a documented and implemented monitoring plan?
<--- Score

63. Are new process steps, standards, and documentation ingrained into normal operations?
<--- Score

64. Are pertinent alerts monitored, analyzed and distributed to appropriate personnel?
<--- Score

65. How do your controls stack up?
<--- Score

66. What other systems, operations, processes, and infrastructures (hiring practices, staffing, training,

incentives/rewards, metrics/dashboards/scorecards, etc.) need updates, additions, changes, or deletions in order to facilitate knowledge transfer and improvements?

<--- Score

67. What do you measure to verify effectiveness gains?

<--- Score

68. Who is the Firewall Knowledge process owner?

<--- Score

69. How will you measure your QA plan's effectiveness?

<--- Score

70. What are the known security controls?

<--- Score

71. Is there a transfer of ownership and knowledge to process owner and process team tasked with the responsibilities.

<--- Score

72. What key inputs and outputs are being measured on an ongoing basis?

<--- Score

73. What is your theory of human motivation, and how does your compensation plan fit with that view?

<--- Score

74. Is knowledge gained on process shared and institutionalized?

<--- Score

75. Is reporting being used or needed?
<--- Score

76. How will the day-to-day responsibilities for monitoring and continual improvement be transferred from the improvement team to the process owner?
<--- Score

77. Is there a control plan in place for sustaining improvements (short and long-term)?
<--- Score

78. Do you monitor the effectiveness of your Firewall Knowledge activities?
<--- Score

Add up total points for this section:
_____ = Total points for this section

Divided by: _____ (number of statements answered) = _____
Average score for this section

Transfer your score to the Firewall Knowledge Index at the beginning of the Self-Assessment.

CRITERION #7: SUSTAIN:

INTENT: Retain the benefits.

In my belief, the answer to this question is clearly defined:

5 Strongly Agree

4 Agree

3 Neutral

2 Disagree

1 Strongly Disagree

1. Are all key stakeholders present at all Structured Walkthroughs?
<--- Score

2. Who do you think the world wants your organization to be?
<--- Score

3. How can you become more high-tech but still be high touch?
<--- Score

4. Can you break it down?
<--- Score

5. What Firewall Knowledge skills are most important?
<--- Score

6. How do you keep the momentum going?
<--- Score

7. At what moment would you think; Will I get fired?
<--- Score

8. Are you maintaining a past–present–future perspective throughout the Firewall Knowledge discussion?
<--- Score

9. What is your BATNA (best alternative to a negotiated agreement)?
<--- Score

10. What are the barriers to increased Firewall Knowledge production?
<--- Score

11. What must you excel at?
<--- Score

12. What relationships among Firewall Knowledge trends do you perceive?
<--- Score

13. Is it economical; do you have the time and money?
<--- Score

14. Are you making progress, and are you making progress as Firewall Knowledge leaders?
<--- Score

15. What information is critical to your organization that your executives are ignoring?
<--- Score

16. Why do and why don't your customers like your organization?
<--- Score

17. How do you engage the workforce, in addition to satisfying them?
<--- Score

18. Are you / should you be revolutionary or evolutionary?
<--- Score

19. Who is responsible for errors?
<--- Score

20. What are the long-term Firewall Knowledge goals?
<--- Score

21. What trouble can you get into?
<--- Score

22. What have been your experiences in defining long range Firewall Knowledge goals?
<--- Score

23. How do you create buy-in?
<--- Score

24. What was the last experiment you ran?
<--- Score

25. Are there any disadvantages to implementing Firewall Knowledge? There might be some that are less obvious?
<--- Score

26. How do you manage Firewall Knowledge Knowledge Management (KM)?
<--- Score

27. Who will provide the final approval of Firewall Knowledge deliverables?
<--- Score

28. Why not do Firewall Knowledge?
<--- Score

29. Political -is anyone trying to undermine this project?
<--- Score

30. What goals did you miss?
<--- Score

31. How do senior leaders deploy your organizations vision and values through your leadership system, to the workforce, to key suppliers and partners, and to customers and other stakeholders, as appropriate?
<--- Score

32. Who are four people whose careers you have enhanced?
<--- Score

33. What are internal and external Firewall Knowledge relations?

<--- Score

34. Why should you adopt a Firewall Knowledge framework?

<--- Score

35. What is the recommended frequency of auditing?

<--- Score

36. What is the purpose of Firewall Knowledge in relation to the mission?

<--- Score

37. What are strategies for increasing support and reducing opposition?

<--- Score

38. If your company went out of business tomorrow, would anyone who doesn't get a paycheck here care?

<--- Score

39. What potential megatrends could make your business model obsolete?

<--- Score

40. What management system can you use to leverage the Firewall Knowledge experience, ideas, and concerns of the people closest to the work to be done?

<--- Score

41. What are your personal philosophies regarding Firewall Knowledge and how do they influence your work?

<--- Score

42. Which models, tools and techniques are
necessary?
<--- Score

43. What current systems have to be understood and/
or changed?
<--- Score

44. What is a feasible sequencing of reform initiatives
over time?
<--- Score

45. What should you stop doing?
<--- Score

46. Instead of going to current contacts for new ideas,
what if you reconnected with dormant contacts--
the people you used to know? If you were going
reactivate a dormant tie, who would it be?
<--- Score

47. How do you transition from the baseline to the
target?
<--- Score

48. Are you paying enough attention to the partners
your company depends on to succeed?
<--- Score

49. Who are your customers?
<--- Score

50. How do you track customer value, profitability
or financial return, organizational success, and

sustainability?
<--- Score

51. Do you know what you are doing? And who do you call if you don't?
<--- Score

52. How does Firewall Knowledge integrate with other business initiatives?
<--- Score

53. If you had to rebuild your organization without any traditional competitive advantages (i.e., no killer a technology, promising research, innovative product/ service delivery model, etc.), how would your people have to approach their work and collaborate together in order to create the necessary conditions for success?
<--- Score

54. What are the business goals Firewall Knowledge is aiming to achieve?
<--- Score

55. What are the key enablers to make this Firewall Knowledge move?
<--- Score

56. Think of your Firewall Knowledge project, what are the main functions?
<--- Score

57. How important is Firewall Knowledge to the user organizations mission?
<--- Score

58. Is the Firewall Knowledge organization completing tasks effectively and efficiently?
<--- Score

59. Do you know who is a friend or a foe?
<--- Score

60. Who else should you help?
<--- Score

61. What threat is Firewall Knowledge addressing?
<--- Score

62. Is your basic point _____ or _____?
<--- Score

63. What are you trying to prove to yourself, and how might it be hijacking your life and business success?
<--- Score

64. Are you relevant? Will you be relevant five years from now? Ten?
<--- Score

65. How can you incorporate support to ensure safe and effective use of Firewall Knowledge into the services that you provide?
<--- Score

66. How is implementation research currently incorporated into each of your goals?
<--- Score

67. What are the essentials of internal Firewall Knowledge management?
<--- Score

68. What Firewall Knowledge modifications can you make work for you?
<--- Score

69. Are new benefits received and understood?
<--- Score

70. Why is Firewall Knowledge important for you now?
<--- Score

71. What will drive Firewall Knowledge change?
<--- Score

72. What are the gaps in your knowledge and experience?
<--- Score

73. Is maximizing Firewall Knowledge protection the same as minimizing Firewall Knowledge loss?
<--- Score

74. What projects are going on in the organization today, and what resources are those projects using from the resource pools?
<--- Score

75. What are the usability implications of Firewall Knowledge actions?
<--- Score

76. Has implementation been effective in reaching specified objectives so far?
<--- Score

77. Who do we want your customers to become?

<--- Score

78. Are assumptions made in Firewall Knowledge stated explicitly?
<--- Score

79. How can you negotiate Firewall Knowledge successfully with a stubborn boss, an irate client, or a deceitful coworker?
<--- Score

80. What would you recommend your friend do if he/she were facing this dilemma?
<--- Score

81. Do you have the right capabilities and capacities?
<--- Score

82. Did your employees make progress today?
<--- Score

83. How are you doing compared to your industry?
<--- Score

84. If no one would ever find out about your accomplishments, how would you lead differently?
<--- Score

85. Do you have an implicit bias for capital investments over people investments?
<--- Score

86. Who are the key stakeholders?
<--- Score

87. What is the overall business strategy?

<--- Score

88. If your customer were your grandmother, would you tell her to buy what you're selling?
<--- Score

89. Who uses your product in ways you never expected?
<--- Score

90. Can you do all this work?
<--- Score

91. Can the schedule be done in the given time?
<--- Score

92. Do Firewall Knowledge rules make a reasonable demand on a users capabilities?
<--- Score

93. What is the estimated value of the project?
<--- Score

94. Do you think you know, or do you know you know ?
<--- Score

95. Who do you want your customers to become?
<--- Score

96. How do you proactively clarify deliverables and Firewall Knowledge quality expectations?
<--- Score

97. What trophy do you want on your mantle?
<--- Score

98. What does your signature ensure?
<--- Score

99. If you had to leave your organization for a year and the only communication you could have with employees/colleagues was a single paragraph, what would you write?
<--- Score

100. Do you say no to customers for no reason?
<--- Score

101. How do you provide a safe environment -physically and emotionally?
<--- Score

102. What kind of crime could a potential new hire have committed that would not only not disqualify him/her from being hired by your organization, but would actually indicate that he/she might be a particularly good fit?
<--- Score

103. Have benefits been optimized with all key stakeholders?
<--- Score

104. What is the kind of project structure that would be appropriate for your Firewall Knowledge project, should it be formal and complex, or can it be less formal and relatively simple?
<--- Score

105. How do you make it meaningful in connecting Firewall Knowledge with what users do day-to-day?

<--- Score

106. Is the impact that Firewall Knowledge has shown?
<--- Score

107. Are you changing as fast as the world around you?
<--- Score

108. What unique value proposition (UVP) do you offer?
<--- Score

109. What is your competitive advantage?
<--- Score

110. How do you govern and fulfill your societal responsibilities?
<--- Score

111. Do you feel that more should be done in the Firewall Knowledge area?
<--- Score

112. Why should people listen to you?
<--- Score

113. Why is it important to have senior management support for a Firewall Knowledge project?
<--- Score

114. Is there any reason to believe the opposite of my current belief?
<--- Score

115. Which functions and people interact with the supplier and or customer?
<--- Score

116. Who will determine interim and final deadlines?
<--- Score

117. Do you have past Firewall Knowledge successes?
<--- Score

118. How do you stay inspired?
<--- Score

119. What are the rules and assumptions your industry operates under? What if the opposite were true?
<--- Score

120. What is effective Firewall Knowledge?
<--- Score

121. What business benefits will Firewall Knowledge goals deliver if achieved?
<--- Score

122. Operational - will it work?
<--- Score

123. What is the overall talent health of your organization as a whole at senior levels, and for each organization reporting to a member of the Senior Leadership Team?
<--- Score

124. If you weren't already in this business, would you enter it today? And if not, what are you going to do about it?

<--- Score

125. What is it like to work for you?
<--- Score

126. Who have you, as a company, historically been when you've been at your best?
<--- Score

127. How do you keep records, of what?
<--- Score

128. Who is the main stakeholder, with ultimate responsibility for driving Firewall Knowledge forward?
<--- Score

129. How will you ensure you get what you expected?
<--- Score

130. Which Firewall Knowledge goals are the most important?
<--- Score

131. How do you set Firewall Knowledge stretch targets and how do you get people to not only participate in setting these stretch targets but also that they strive to achieve these?
<--- Score

132. Will it be accepted by users?
<--- Score

133. Can you maintain your growth without detracting from the factors that have contributed to your success?
<--- Score

134. In retrospect, of the projects that you pulled the plug on, what percent do you wish had been allowed to keep going, and what percent do you wish had ended earlier?
<--- Score

135. Who, on the executive team or the board, has spoken to a customer recently?
<--- Score

136. Whom among your colleagues do you trust, and for what?
<--- Score

137. What are the short and long-term Firewall Knowledge goals?
<--- Score

138. Who will be responsible for deciding whether Firewall Knowledge goes ahead or not after the initial investigations?
<--- Score

139. Ask yourself: how would you do this work if you only had one staff member to do it?
<--- Score

140. When you map the key players in your own work and the types/domains of relationships with them, which relationships do you find easy and which challenging, and why?
<--- Score

141. If there were zero limitations, what would you do differently?

<--- Score

142. Which individuals, teams or departments will be involved in Firewall Knowledge?
<--- Score

143. What is the funding source for this project?
<--- Score

144. How likely is it that a customer would recommend your company to a friend or colleague?
<--- Score

145. How much contingency will be available in the budget?
<--- Score

146. What are you challenging?
<--- Score

147. How do you cross-sell and up-sell your Firewall Knowledge success?
<--- Score

148. How will you motivate the stakeholders with the least vested interest?
<--- Score

149. How do you maintain Firewall Knowledge's Integrity?
<--- Score

150. Is a Firewall Knowledge team work effort in place?
<--- Score

151. What are the potential basics of Firewall Knowledge fraud?

<--- Score

152. What is your question? Why?

<--- Score

153. What is the source of the strategies for Firewall Knowledge strengthening and reform?

<--- Score

154. What is the craziest thing you can do?

<--- Score

155. If you got fired and a new hire took your place, what would she do different?

<--- Score

156. Is there any existing Firewall Knowledge governance structure?

<--- Score

157. How do you foster innovation?

<--- Score

158. What are current Firewall Knowledge paradigms?

<--- Score

159. Are the assumptions believable and achievable?

<--- Score

160. To whom do you add value?

<--- Score

161. Have new benefits been realized?

<--- Score

162. What knowledge, skills and characteristics mark a good Firewall Knowledge project manager?
<--- Score

163. Among your stronger employees, how many see themselves at the company in three years? How many would leave for a 10 percent raise from another company?
<--- Score

164. Who is responsible for ensuring appropriate resources (time, people and money) are allocated to Firewall Knowledge?
<--- Score

165. What are the top 3 things at the forefront of your Firewall Knowledge agendas for the next 3 years?
<--- Score

166. Were lessons learned captured and communicated?
<--- Score

167. What you are going to do to affect the numbers?
<--- Score

168. What new services of functionality will be implemented next with Firewall Knowledge ?
<--- Score

169. Is Firewall Knowledge dependent on the successful delivery of a current project?
<--- Score

170. If you were responsible for initiating and

implementing major changes in your organization, what steps might you take to ensure acceptance of those changes?
<--- Score

171. What do we do when new problems arise?
<--- Score

172. Are you satisfied with your current role? If not, what is missing from it?
<--- Score

173. What are your most important goals for the strategic Firewall Knowledge objectives?
<--- Score

174. How much does Firewall Knowledge help?
<--- Score

175. Who is responsible for Firewall Knowledge?
<--- Score

176. How do you assess the Firewall Knowledge pitfalls that are inherent in implementing it?
<--- Score

177. What are specific Firewall Knowledge rules to follow?
<--- Score

178. What are the success criteria that will indicate that Firewall Knowledge objectives have been met and the benefits delivered?
<--- Score

179. How do you know if you are successful?

<--- Score

180. Is your strategy driving your strategy? Or is the way in which you allocate resources driving your strategy?
<--- Score

181. How do you foster the skills, knowledge, talents, attributes, and characteristics you want to have?
<--- Score

182. What would have to be true for the option on the table to be the best possible choice?
<--- Score

183. How do you accomplish your long range Firewall Knowledge goals?
<--- Score

184. What will be the consequences to the stakeholder (financial, reputation etc) if Firewall Knowledge does not go ahead or fails to deliver the objectives?
<--- Score

185. When information truly is ubiquitous, when reach and connectivity are completely global, when computing resources are infinite, and when a whole new set of impossibilities are not only possible, but happening, what will that do to your business?
<--- Score

186. What may be the consequences for the performance of an organization if all stakeholders are not consulted regarding Firewall Knowledge?
<--- Score

187. In the past year, what have you done (or could you have done) to increase the accurate perception of your company/brand as ethical and honest?
<--- Score

188. Do you have enough freaky customers in your portfolio pushing you to the limit day in and day out?
<--- Score

189. What is your formula for success in Firewall Knowledge ?
<--- Score

190. Do you see more potential in people than they do in themselves?
<--- Score

191. How do you lead with Firewall Knowledge in mind?
<--- Score

192. What happens if you do not have enough funding?
<--- Score

193. How do you listen to customers to obtain actionable information?
<--- Score

Add up total points for this section:
_ _ _ _ _ = Total points for this section

Divided by: _ _ _ _ _ _ (number of statements answered) = _ _ _ _ _ _
Average score for this section

Transfer your score to the Firewall
Knowledge Index at the beginning of
the Self-Assessment.

Firewall Knowledge and Managing Projects, Criteria for Project Managers:

1.0 Initiating Process Group: Firewall Knowledge

1. Who is performing the work of the Firewall Knowledge project?

2. How well did the chosen processes fit the needs of the Firewall Knowledge project?

3. When must it be done?

4. At which cmmi level are software processes documented, standardized, and integrated into a standard to-be practiced process for your organization?

5. During which stage of Risk planning are risks prioritized based on probability and impact?

6. What were things that you need to improve?

7. Who are the Firewall Knowledge project stakeholders?

8. Are you just doing busywork to pass the time?

9. How can you make your needs known?

10. What areas were overlooked on this Firewall Knowledge project?

11. What areas does the group agree are the biggest success on the Firewall Knowledge project?

12. What do they need to know about the Firewall

Knowledge project?

13. When are the deliverables to be generated in each phase?

14. Where must it be done?

15. What were things that you did well, and could improve, and how?

16. How will you do it?

17. Although the Firewall Knowledge project manager does not directly manage procurement and contracting activities, who does manage procurement and contracting activities in your organization then if not the PM?

18. Have the stakeholders identified all individual requirements pertaining to business process?

19. At which stage, in a typical Firewall Knowledge project do stake holders have maximum influence?

20. Who is involved in each phase?

1.1 Project Charter: Firewall Knowledge

21. Must Have?

22. Who is the Firewall Knowledge project Manager?

23. Name and describe the elements that deal with providing the detail?

24. Why is it important?

25. How will you know a change is an improvement?

26. What changes can you make to improve?

27. What are the deliverables?

28. What metrics could you look at?

29. Who are the stakeholders?

30. Are there special technology requirements?

31. What are the assumptions?

32. Is it an improvement over existing products?

33. What barriers do you predict to your success?

34. How high should you set your goals?

35. Why Outsource?

36. Does the Firewall Knowledge project need to consider any special capacity or capability issues?

37. Where and how does the team fit within your organization structure?

38. Avoid costs, improve service, and/ or comply with a mandate?

39. Market – identify products market, including whether it is outside of the objective: what is the purpose of the program or Firewall Knowledge project?

40. Why executive support?

1.2 Stakeholder Register: Firewall Knowledge

41. Who wants to talk about Security?

42. Who is managing stakeholder engagement?

43. What & Why?

44. What are the major Firewall Knowledge project milestones requiring communications or providing communications opportunities?

45. What is the power of the stakeholder?

46. How will reports be created?

47. Is your organization ready for change?

48. How big is the gap?

49. How should employers make voices heard?

50. What opportunities exist to provide communications?

51. How much influence do they have on the Firewall Knowledge project?

1.3 Stakeholder Analysis Matrix: Firewall Knowledge

52. Volumes, production, economies?

53. How do rules, behaviors affect stakes?

54. Continuity, supply chain robustness?

55. Disadvantages of proposition?

56. Niche target markets?

57. How to measure the achievement of the Outputs?

58. Supporters; who are the supporters?

59. Sustainable financial backing?

60. What is your organizations competitors doing?

61. What do people from other organizations see as your organizations weaknesses?

62. Does your organization have bad debt or cash-flow problems?

63. Is there a clear description of the scope of practice of the Firewall Knowledge projects educators?

64. What mechanisms are proposed to monitor and measure Firewall Knowledge project performance in terms of social development outcomes?

65. Who can contribute financial or technical resources towards the work?

66. Geographical, export, import?

67. What do people from other organizations see as your strengths?

68. Are there people who ise voices or interests in the issue may not be heard?

69. Industry or lifestyle trends?

70. Is changing technology threatening your organizations position?

71. Vulnerable groups; who are the vulnerable groups that might be affected by the Firewall Knowledge project?

2.0 Planning Process Group: Firewall Knowledge

72. Will you be replaced?

73. What factors are contributing to progress or delay in the achievement of products and results?

74. To what extent is the program helping to influence your organizations policy framework?

75. Have operating capacities been created and/or reinforced in partners?

76. In which Firewall Knowledge project management process group is the detailed Firewall Knowledge project budget created?

77. To what extent and in what ways are the Firewall Knowledge project contributing to progress towards organizational reform?

78. Who are the Firewall Knowledge project stakeholders?

79. How can you tell when you are done?

80. What makes your Firewall Knowledge project successful?

81. If task x starts two days late, what is the effect on the Firewall Knowledge project end date?

82. Will the products created live up to the necessary quality?

83. Is the Firewall Knowledge project making progress in helping to achieve the set results?

84. What is the critical path for this Firewall Knowledge project, and what is the duration of the critical path?

85. In what ways can the governance of the Firewall Knowledge project be improved so that it has greater likelihood of achieving future sustainability?

86. The Firewall Knowledge project charter is created in which Firewall Knowledge project management process group?

87. What input will you be required to provide the Firewall Knowledge project team?

88. Is the schedule for the set products being met?

89. How are the principles of aid effectiveness (ownership, alignment, management for development results and mutual responsibility) being applied in the Firewall Knowledge project?

90. What do you need to do?

91. What is the difference between the early schedule and late schedule?

2.1 Project Management Plan: Firewall Knowledge

92. Are the existing and future without-plan conditions reasonable and appropriate?

93. What happened during the process that you found interesting?

94. Are the proposed Firewall Knowledge project purposes different than a previously authorized Firewall Knowledge project?

95. What is Firewall Knowledge project scope management?

96. Is the engineering content at a feasibility level-of-detail, and is it sufficiently complete, to provide an adequate basis for the baseline cost estimate?

97. Is there an incremental analysis/cost effectiveness analysis of proposed mitigation features based on an approved method and using an accepted model?

98. Will you add a schedule and diagram?

99. What went wrong?

100. Why do you manage integration?

101. What if, for example, the positive direction and vision of your organization causes expected trends to change resulting in greater need than expected?

102. What is the business need?

103. If the Firewall Knowledge project management plan is a comprehensive document that guides you in Firewall Knowledge project execution and control, then what should it NOT contain?

104. Is the appropriate plan selected based on your organizations objectives and evaluation criteria expressed in Principles and Guidelines policies?

105. Does the implementation plan have an appropriate division of responsibilities?

106. What did not work so well?

107. Has the selected plan been formulated using cost effectiveness and incremental analysis techniques?

108. Development trends and opportunities. What if the positive direction and vision of your organization causes expected trends to change?

109. What goes into your Firewall Knowledge project Charter?

110. What are the known stakeholder requirements?

2.2 Scope Management Plan: Firewall Knowledge

111. Are metrics used to evaluate and manage Vendors?

112. Are the schedule estimates reasonable given the Firewall Knowledge project?

113. Has process improvement efforts been completed before requirements efforts begin?

114. Is there a set of procedures defining the scope, procedures, and deliverables defining quality control?

115. Are all key components of a Quality Assurance Plan present?

116. Function of the configuration control board?

117. Are measurements and feedback mechanisms incorporated in tracking work effort & refining work estimating techniques?

118. Is there a formal process for updating the Firewall Knowledge project baseline?

119. Has the Firewall Knowledge project approach and development strategy of the Firewall Knowledge project been defined, documented and accepted by the appropriate stakeholders?

120. How do you handle uncertainty or conflict?

121. Do you document disagreements and work towards resolutions?

122. Why do you need to manage scope?

123. What are the risks that could significantly affect the scope of the Firewall Knowledge project?

124. Are software metrics formally captured, analyzed and used as a basis for other Firewall Knowledge project estimates?

125. Is mitigation authorized or recommended?

126. Deliverables -are the deliverables tangible and verifiable?

127. Timeline and milestones?

128. During what part of the PM process is the Firewall Knowledge project scope statement created?

129. Describe how the deliverables will be verified against the Firewall Knowledge project scope. To whom will the deliverables be first presented for inspection and verification?

130. Are funding resource estimates sufficiently detailed and documented for use in planning and tracking the Firewall Knowledge project?

2.3 Requirements Management Plan: Firewall Knowledge

131. Controlling Firewall Knowledge project requirements involves monitoring the status of the Firewall Knowledge project requirements and managing changes to the requirements. Who is responsible for monitoring and tracking the Firewall Knowledge project requirements?

132. Is the system software (non-operating system) new to the IT Firewall Knowledge project team?

133. Is infrastructure setup part of your Firewall Knowledge project?

134. Are actual resources expenditures versus planned expenditures acceptable?

135. Are actual resource expenditures versus planned still acceptable?

136. Did you use declarative statements?

137. How will you communicate scheduled tasks to other team members?

138. Is it new or replacing an existing business system or process?

139. How will the requirements become prioritized?

140. What are you trying to do?

141. What is the earliest finish date for this Firewall Knowledge project if it is scheduled to start on ...?

142. Will you document changes to requirements?

143. Who will approve the requirements (and if multiple approvers, in what order)?

144. Does the Firewall Knowledge project have a Change Control process?

145. Who has the authority to reject Firewall Knowledge project requirements?

146. Should you include sub-activities?

147. Who will initially review the Firewall Knowledge project work or products to ensure it meets the applicable acceptance criteria?

148. Are all the stakeholders ready for the transition into the user community?

149. Do you expect stakeholders to be cooperative?

150. Will you perform a Requirements Risk assessment and develop a plan to deal with risks?

2.4 Requirements Documentation: Firewall Knowledge

151. What if the system wasn t implemented?

152. How do you get the user to tell you what they want?

153. Is the requirement properly understood?

154. Validity. does the system provide the functions which best support the customers needs?

155. The problem with gathering requirements is right there in the word gathering. What images does it conjure?

156. Do your constraints stand?

157. How linear / iterative is your Requirements Gathering process (or will it be)?

158. Where do you define what is a customer, what are the attributes of customer?

159. What is your Elevator Speech?

160. Is your business case still valid?

161. Can the requirements be checked?

162. Who is interacting with the system?

163. What are the attributes of a customer?

164. What images does it conjure?

165. What kind of entity is a problem ?

166. What is effective documentation?

167. Consistency. are there any requirements conflicts?

168. Where do system and software requirements come from, what are sources?

169. How much does requirements engineering cost?

170. What are the acceptance criteria?

2.5 Requirements Traceability Matrix: Firewall Knowledge

171. Why do you manage scope?

172. What is the WBS?

173. How will it affect the stakeholders personally in their career?

174. How do you manage scope?

175. How small is small enough?

176. Describe the process for approving requirements so they can be added to the traceability matrix and Firewall Knowledge project work can be performed. Will the Firewall Knowledge project requirements become approved in writing?

177. What percentage of Firewall Knowledge projects are producing traceability matrices between requirements and other work products?

178. Will you use a Requirements Traceability Matrix?

179. Is there a requirements traceability process in place?

180. What are the chronologies, contingencies, consequences, criteria?

181. Why use a WBS?

182. Do you have a clear understanding of all subcontracts in place?

2.6 Project Scope Statement: Firewall Knowledge

183. Will all Firewall Knowledge project issues be unconditionally tracked through the issue resolution process?

184. If there is an independent oversight contractor, have they signed off on the Firewall Knowledge project Plan?

185. Is there a Quality Assurance Plan documented and filed?

186. Will statistics related to QA be collected, trends analyzed, and problems raised as issues?

187. Is the plan for Firewall Knowledge project resources adequate?

188. Is the change control process documented and on file?

189. Did your Firewall Knowledge project ask for this?

190. How often will scope changes be reviewed?

191. What is the most common tool for helping define the detail?

192. Were key Firewall Knowledge project stakeholders brought into the Firewall Knowledge project Plan?

193. Is there a Change Management Board?

194. What are the defined meeting materials?

195. Will the qa related information be reported regularly as part of the status reporting mechanisms?

196. Is your organization structure appropriate for the Firewall Knowledge projects size and complexity?

197. Is this process communicated to the customer and team members?

198. Has everyone approved the Firewall Knowledge projects scope statement?

199. What is change?

200. What went right?

201. Is there a process (test plans, inspections, reviews) defined for verifying outputs for each task?

202. Elements that deal with providing the detail?

2.7 Assumption and Constraint Log: Firewall Knowledge

203. What strengths do you have?

204. Is the current scope of the Firewall Knowledge project substantially different than that originally defined in the approved Firewall Knowledge project plan?

205. How are new requirements or changes to requirements identified?

206. Do the requirements meet the standards of correctness, completeness, consistency, accuracy, and readability?

207. Are there ways to reduce the time it takes to get something approved?

208. What other teams / processes would be impacted by changes to the current process, and how?

209. Has the approach and development strategy of the Firewall Knowledge project been defined, documented and accepted by the appropriate stakeholders?

210. Violation trace: why ?

211. Are formal code reviews conducted?

212. What weaknesses do you have?

213. Are there procedures in place to effectively manage interdependencies with other Firewall Knowledge projects / systems?

214. Were the system requirements formally reviewed prior to initiating the design phase?

215. Is the process working, and people are not executing in compliance of the process?

216. What is positive about the current process?

217. Do you know what your customers expectations are regarding this process?

218. Have all necessary approvals been obtained?

219. How can constraints be violated?

220. Have the scope, objectives, costs, benefits and impacts been communicated to all involved and/or impacted stakeholders and work groups?

221. Have all stakeholders been identified?

222. Are there processes defining how software will be developed including development methods, overall timeline for development, software product standards, and traceability?

2.8 Work Breakdown Structure: Firewall Knowledge

223. Who has to do it?

224. How will you and your Firewall Knowledge project team define the Firewall Knowledge projects scope and work breakdown structure?

225. Is it still viable?

226. What is the probability of completing the Firewall Knowledge project in less that xx days?

227. Is the work breakdown structure (wbs) defined and is the scope of the Firewall Knowledge project clear with assigned deliverable owners?

228. How much detail?

229. How far down?

230. When do you stop?

231. When would you develop a Work Breakdown Structure?

232. Is it a change in scope?

233. How big is a work-package?

234. What is the probability that the Firewall Knowledge project duration will exceed xx weeks?

235. Can you make it?

236. Do you need another level?

237. How many levels?

238. What has to be done?

239. Why would you develop a Work Breakdown Structure?

240. Why is it useful?

241. Where does it take place?

242. When does it have to be done?

2.9 WBS Dictionary: Firewall Knowledge

243. What size should a work package be?

244. Are meaningful indicators identified for use in measuring the status of cost and schedule performance?

245. Is undistributed budget limited to contract effort which cannot yet be planned to CWBS elements at or below the level specified for reporting to the Government?

246. Are overhead cost budgets (or Firewall Knowledge projections) established on a facility-wide basis at least annually for the life of the contract?

247. Are the bases and rates for allocating costs from each indirect pool to commercial work consistent with the already stated used to allocate corresponding costs to Government contracts?

248. Do the lines of authority for incurring indirect costs correspond to the lines of responsibility for management control of the same components of costs?

249. Contractor financial periods; for example, annual?

250. Does the sum of all work package budgets plus planning packages within control accounts equal

the budgets assigned to the already stated control accounts?

251. Does the contractors system description or procedures require that the performance measurement baseline plus management reserve equal the contract budget base?

252. Are records maintained to show full accountability for all material purchased for the contract, including the residual inventory?

253. Are data elements (BCWS, BCWP, and ACWP) progressively summarized from the detail level to the contract level through the CWBS?

254. Are estimates developed by Firewall Knowledge project personnel coordinated with the already stated responsible for overall management to determine whether required resources will be available according to revised planning?

255. Are the wbs and organizational levels for application of the Firewall Knowledge projected overhead costs identified?

256. Budgeted cost for work performed?

257. Are records maintained to show how management reserves are used?

258. Are budgets or values assigned to work packages and planning packages in terms of dollars, hours, or other measurable units?

259. Does the scheduling system provide for the

identification of work progress against technical and other milestones, and also provide for forecasts of completion dates of scheduled work?

260. Is data disseminated to the contractors management timely, accurate, and usable?

2.10 Schedule Management Plan: Firewall Knowledge

261. Is the development plan and/or process documented?

262. Are written status reports provided on a designated frequent basis?

263. Are changes in scope (deliverable commitments) agreed to by all affected groups & individuals?

264. Are cause and effect determined for risks when they occur?

265. Has your organization readiness assessment been conducted?

266. What threats might prevent you from getting there?

267. Are risk triggers captured?

268. Who is responsible for estimating the activity durations?

269. Are there checklists created to determine if all quality processes are followed?

270. Has the ims been resource-loaded and are assigned resources reasonable and available?

271. Is your organization certified as a supplier,

wholesaler and/or regular dealer?

272. Are tasks tracked by hours?

273. Are the schedule estimates reasonable given the Firewall Knowledge project?

274. Does the Firewall Knowledge project have a formal Firewall Knowledge project Charter?

275. Have Firewall Knowledge project success criteria been defined?

276. Time for overtime?

277. Are there any activities or deliverables being added or gold-plated that could be dropped or scaled back without falling short of the original requirement?

278. Have all team members been part of identifying risks?

279. Quality assurance overheads?

280. Does the time Firewall Knowledge projection include an amount for contingencies (time reserves)?

2.11 Activity List: Firewall Knowledge

281. How do you determine the late start (LS) for each activity?

282. For other activities, how much delay can be tolerated?

283. Where will it be performed?

284. What did not go as well?

285. In what sequence?

286. Are the required resources available or need to be acquired?

287. Who will perform the work?

288. What are the critical bottleneck activities?

289. Can you determine the activity that must finish, before this activity can start?

290. The wbs is developed as part of a joint planning session. and how do you know that youhave done this right?

291. How can the Firewall Knowledge project be displayed graphically to better visualize the activities?

292. Is there anything planned that does not need to be here?

293. How detailed should a Firewall Knowledge project get?

294. Is infrastructure setup part of your Firewall Knowledge project?

295. What is the LF and LS for each activity?

296. What is the probability the Firewall Knowledge project can be completed in xx weeks?

297. How should ongoing costs be monitored to try to keep the Firewall Knowledge project within budget?

298. How much slack is available in the Firewall Knowledge project?

2.12 Activity Attributes: Firewall Knowledge

299. What is the general pattern here?

300. How else could the items be grouped?

301. How difficult will it be to complete specific activities on this Firewall Knowledge project?

302. How much activity detail is required?

303. Where else does it apply?

304. Would you consider either of corresponding activities an outlier?

305. How many resources do you need to complete the work scope within a limit of X number of days?

306. Have you identified the Activity Leveling Priority code value on each activity?

307. Which method produces the more accurate cost assignment?

308. How difficult will it be to do specific activities on this Firewall Knowledge project?

309. How do you manage time?

310. Can more resources be added?

311. What conclusions/generalizations can you draw from this?

312. Activity: what is In the Bag?

313. What activity do you think you should spend the most time on?

314. Do you feel very comfortable with your prediction?

315. What is missing?

316. Has management defined a definite timeframe for the turnaround or Firewall Knowledge project window?

317. Is there a trend during the year?

2.13 Milestone List: Firewall Knowledge

318. How will you get the word out to customers?

319. How will the milestone be verified?

320. Level of the Innovation?

321. Loss of key staff?

322. Do you foresee any technical risks or developmental challenges?

323. What would happen if a delivery of material was one week late?

324. Political effects?

325. Usps (unique selling points)?

326. Legislative effects?

327. What has been done so far?

328. How soon can the activity start?

329. Sustaining internal capabilities?

330. What is the market for your technology, product or service?

331. It is to be a narrative text providing the crucial

aspects of your Firewall Knowledge project proposal answering what, who, how, when and where?

332. Can you derive how soon can the whole Firewall Knowledge project finish?

333. Calculate how long can activity be delayed?

334. Insurmountable weaknesses?

335. Vital contracts and partners?

2.14 Network Diagram: Firewall Knowledge

336. What to do and When?

337. What is your organizations history in doing similar activities?

338. Are you on time?

339. What is the completion time?

340. How confident can you be in your milestone dates and the delivery date?

341. Review the logical flow of the network diagram. Take a look at which activities you have first and then sequence the activities. Do they make sense?

342. Are the required resources available?

343. What activities must follow this activity?

344. What are the Key Success Factors?

345. Are the gantt chart and/or network diagram updated periodically and used to assess the overall Firewall Knowledge project timetable?

346. What job or jobs could run concurrently?

347. Will crashing x weeks return more in benefits than it costs?

348. What job or jobs follow it?

349. Planning: who, how long, what to do?

350. What controls the start and finish of a job?

351. Can you calculate the confidence level?

352. How difficult will it be to do specific activities on this Firewall Knowledge project?

353. Why must you schedule milestones, such as reviews, throughout the Firewall Knowledge project?

354. What activities must occur simultaneously with this activity?

355. What is the probability of completing the Firewall Knowledge project in less that xx days?

2.15 Activity Resource Requirements: Firewall Knowledge

356. Why do you do that?

357. Organizational Applicability?

358. What is the Work Plan Standard?

359. How many signatures do you require on a check and does this match what is in your policy and procedures?

360. Anything else?

361. When does monitoring begin?

362. How do you handle petty cash?

363. Are there unresolved issues that need to be addressed?

364. Which logical relationship does the PDM use most often?

365. What are constraints that you might find during the Human Resource Planning process?

366. Do you use tools like decomposition and rolling-wave planning to produce the activity list and other outputs?

367. Other support in specific areas?

2.16 Resource Breakdown Structure: Firewall Knowledge

368. Who will be used as a Firewall Knowledge project team member?

369. What can you do to improve productivity?

370. Who is allowed to see what data about which resources?

371. The list could probably go on, but, the thing that you would most like to know is, How long & How much?

372. Why is this important?

373. Who is allowed to perform which functions?

374. What is each stakeholders desired outcome for the Firewall Knowledge project?

375. What defines a successful Firewall Knowledge project?

376. What is the primary purpose of the human resource plan?

377. Goals for the Firewall Knowledge project. What is each stakeholders desired outcome for the Firewall Knowledge project?

378. Who will use the system?

379. What is the difference between % Complete and % work?

380. Who needs what information?

381. What is the number one predictor of a groups productivity?

382. Why time management?

383. Who delivers the information?

2.17 Activity Duration Estimates: Firewall Knowledge

384. What tasks can take place concurrently?

385. Are activity dependencies documented?

386. Are Firewall Knowledge project costs tracked in the general ledger?

387. How can organizations use a weighted decision matrix to evaluate proposals as part of source selection?

388. If Firewall Knowledge project time and cost are not as important as the number of resources used each month, which is the BEST thing to do?

389. Do they make sense?

390. Which types of reports would help provide summary information to senior management?

391. What is the difference between conceptual, application, and evaluative questions?

392. What is the duration of a milestone?

393. Are risks monitored to determine if an event has occurred or if the mitigation was successful?

394. Consider the changes in the job market for information technology workers. How does the

job market and current state of the economy affect human resource management?

395. Consider the common sources of risk on information technology Firewall Knowledge projects and suggestions for managing them. Which suggestions do you find most useful?

396. Are contingency plans created to prepare for risk events to occur?

397. Which suggestions do you find most useful?

398. How many different communications channels does a Firewall Knowledge project team with six people have?

399. What are the main parts of a scope statement?

400. How do functionality, system outputs, performance, reliability, and maintainability requirements affect quality planning?

401. What are the advantages and disadvantages of PERT?

2.18 Duration Estimating Worksheet: Firewall Knowledge

402. When does your organization expect to be able to complete it?

403. Will the Firewall Knowledge project collaborate with the local community and leverage resources?

404. Is the Firewall Knowledge project responsive to community need?

405. What info is needed?

406. How should ongoing costs be monitored to try to keep the Firewall Knowledge project within budget?

407. When do the individual activities need to start and finish?

408. Why estimate costs?

409. Do any colleagues have experience with your organization and/or RFPs?

410. How can the Firewall Knowledge project be displayed graphically to better visualize the activities?

411. Define the work as completely as possible. What work will be included in the Firewall Knowledge project?

412. Small or large Firewall Knowledge project?

413. What is your role?

414. When, then?

415. What is an Average Firewall Knowledge project?

416. Is a construction detail attached (to aid in explanation)?

417. Why estimate time and cost?

2.19 Project Schedule: Firewall Knowledge

418. How closely did the initial Firewall Knowledge project Schedule compare with the actual schedule?

419. Does the condition or event threaten the Firewall Knowledge projects objectives in any ways?

420. Schedule/cost recovery?

421. How effectively were issues able to be resolved without impacting the Firewall Knowledge project Schedule or Budget?

422. Did the final product meet or exceed user expectations?

423. Did the Firewall Knowledge project come in on schedule?

424. Is the structure for tracking the Firewall Knowledge project schedule well defined and assigned to a specific individual?

425. What are you counting on?

426. How do you use schedules?

427. Why do you need to manage Firewall Knowledge project Risk?

428. Why is this particularly bad?

429. Have all Firewall Knowledge project delays been adequately accounted for, communicated to all stakeholders and adjustments made in overall Firewall Knowledge project schedule?

430. What is the most mis-scheduled part of process?

431. Change management required?

432. Eliminate unnecessary activities. Are there activities that came from a template or previous Firewall Knowledge project that are not applicable on this phase of this Firewall Knowledge project?

433. Understand the constraints used in preparing the schedule. Are activities connected because logic dictates the order in which others occur?

434. It allows the Firewall Knowledge project to be delivered on schedule. How Do you Use Schedules?

2.20 Cost Management Plan: Firewall Knowledge

435. Are the appropriate IT resources adequate to meet planned commitments?

436. Similar Firewall Knowledge projects?

437. Was the scope definition used in task sequencing?

438. What is an Acceptance Management Process?

439. Is there an issues management plan in place?

440. Are key risk mitigation strategies added to the Firewall Knowledge project schedule?

441. Is pert / critical path or equivalent methodology being used?

442. Forecasts – how will the cost to complete the Firewall Knowledge project be forecast?

443. Are estimating assumptions and constraints captured?

444. Have the key functions and capabilities been defined and assigned to each release or iteration?

445. Are meeting objectives identified for each meeting?

446. Has a quality assurance plan been developed for the Firewall Knowledge project?

447. Why do you manage cost?

448. Does the detailed work plan match the complexity of tasks with the capabilities of personnel?

449. Resources – how will human resources be scheduled during each phase of the Firewall Knowledge project?

450. Is stakeholder involvement adequate?

451. Scope of work – What is the likelihood and extent of potential future changes to the Firewall Knowledge project scope?

452. Published materials?

453. Milestones – what are the key dates in executing the contract plan?

2.21 Activity Cost Estimates: Firewall Knowledge

454. How many activities should you have?

455. If you are asked to lower your estimate because the price is too high, what are your options?

456. How do you allocate indirect costs to activities?

457. Does the activity rely on a common set of tools to carry it out?

458. How do you treat administrative costs in the activity inventory?

459. Eac -estimate at completion, what is the total job expected to cost?

460. How Award?

461. What is the last item a Firewall Knowledge project manager must do to finalize Firewall Knowledge project close-out?

462. Measurable - are the targets measurable?

463. Is costing method consistent with study goals?

464. What happens if you cannot produce the documentation for the single audit?

465. Vac -variance at completion, how much over/

under budget do you expect to be?

466. How and when do you enter into Firewall Knowledge project Procurement Management?

467. What do you want to know about the stay to know if costs were inappropriately high or low?

468. What is the activity recast of the budget?

469. Can you change your activities?

470. What makes a good activity description?

471. How difficult will it be to do specific tasks on the Firewall Knowledge project?

472. How do you fund change orders?

2.22 Cost Estimating Worksheet: Firewall Knowledge

473. What can be included?

474. What is the estimated labor cost today based upon this information?

475. Does the Firewall Knowledge project provide innovative ways for stakeholders to overcome obstacles or deliver better outcomes?

476. Is it feasible to establish a control group arrangement?

477. Will the Firewall Knowledge project collaborate with the local community and leverage resources?

478. Who is best positioned to know and assist in identifying corresponding factors?

479. Value pocket identification & quantification what are value pockets?

480. Identify the timeframe necessary to monitor progress and collect data to determine how the selected measure has changed?

481. What will others want?

482. What additional Firewall Knowledge project(s) could be initiated as a result of this Firewall Knowledge project?

483. Can a trend be established from historical performance data on the selected measure and are the criteria for using trend analysis or forecasting methods met?

484. Is the Firewall Knowledge project responsive to community need?

485. Ask: are others positioned to know, are others credible, and will others cooperate?

486. What costs are to be estimated?

487. What is the purpose of estimating?

488. How will the results be shared and to whom?

489. What happens to any remaining funds not used?

2.23 Cost Baseline: Firewall Knowledge

490. Will the Firewall Knowledge project fail if the change request is not executed?

491. Has the Firewall Knowledge project documentation been archived or otherwise disposed as described in the Firewall Knowledge project communication plan?

492. What is your organizations history in doing similar tasks?

493. Has the documentation relating to operation and maintenance of the product(s) or service(s) been delivered to, and accepted by, operations management?

494. How fast?

495. What deliverables come first?

496. What is it ?

497. What is cost and Firewall Knowledge project cost management?

498. Does it impact schedule, cost, quality?

499. Review your risk triggers -have your risks changed?

500. How concrete were original objectives?

501. Have the resources used by the Firewall Knowledge project been reassigned to other units or Firewall Knowledge projects?

502. When should cost estimates be developed?

503. Have all the product or service deliverables been accepted by the customer?

504. Have the lessons learned been filed with the Firewall Knowledge project Management Office?

505. Has operations management formally accepted responsibility for operating and maintaining the product(s) or service(s) delivered by the Firewall Knowledge project?

2.24 Quality Management Plan: Firewall Knowledge

506. How do senior leaders create and communicate values and performance expectations?

507. How is staff trained on the recording of field notes?

508. How does your organization maintain a safe and healthy work environment?

509. Methodology followed?

510. How effectively was the Quality Management Plan applied during Firewall Knowledge project Execution?

511. With the five whys method, the team considers why the issue being explored occurred. do others then take that initial answer and ask why?

512. Written by multiple authors and in multiple writing styles?

513. What key performance indicators does your organization use to measure, manage, and improve key processes?

514. How many Firewall Knowledge project staff does this specific process affect?

515. How does your organization decide what to

measure?

516. How does your organization address regulatory, legal, and ethical compliance?

517. What are you trying to accomplish?

518. What is your organizations strategic planning process?

519. How are records kept in the office?

520. What are your key performance measures/ indicators for tracking progress relative to your action plans?

521. Sampling part of task?

522. What methods are used?

523. Can it be done better?

524. How do you ensure that your sampling methods and procedures meet your data needs?

2.25 Quality Metrics: Firewall Knowledge

525. What do you measure?

526. Are there already quality metrics available that detect nonlinear embeddings and trends similar to the users perception?

527. Are there any open risk issues?

528. Did evaluation start on time?

529. How do you calculate corresponding metrics?

530. Has risk analysis been adequately reviewed?

531. What makes a visualization memorable?

532. Can visual measures help you to filter visualizations of interest?

533. What approved evidence based screening tools can be used?

534. What is the benchmark?

535. Can you correlate your quality metrics to profitability?

536. What documentation is required?

537. Which are the right metrics to use?

538. Who is willing to lead?

539. When will the Final Guidance will be issued?

540. Do you know how much profit a 10% decrease in waste would generate?

541. If the defect rate during testing is substantially higher than that of the previous release (or a similar product), then ask: Did you plan for and actually improve testing effectiveness?

542. There are many reasons to shore up quality-related metrics, and what metrics are important?

543. Which report did you use to create the data you are submitting?

544. Should a modifier be included?

2.26 Process Improvement Plan: Firewall Knowledge

545. What personnel are the sponsors for that initiative?

546. Have storage and access mechanisms and procedures been determined?

547. The motive is determined by asking, Why do you want to achieve this goal?

548. What lessons have you learned so far?

549. Does explicit definition of the measures exist?

550. What makes people good SPI coaches?

551. Has a process guide to collect the data been developed?

552. Purpose of goal: the motive is determined by asking, why do you want to achieve this goal?

553. Where do you want to be?

554. What actions are needed to address the problems and achieve the goals?

555. Does your process ensure quality?

556. Have the supporting tools been developed or acquired?

557. What is the return on investment?

558. Are you making progress on the improvement framework?

559. To elicit goal statements, do you ask a question such as, What do you want to achieve?

560. If a process improvement framework is being used, which elements will help the problems and goals listed?

561. Are you meeting the quality standards?

562. Management commitment at all levels?

563. Are you following the quality standards?

564. Has the time line required to move measurement results from the points of collection to databases or users been established?

2.27 Responsibility Assignment Matrix: Firewall Knowledge

565. Who is the Firewall Knowledge project Manager?

566. Does the contractor use objective results, design reviews, and tests to trace schedule?

567. Who is responsible for work and budgets for each wbs?

568. Evaluate the performance of operating organizations?

569. Availability – will the group or the person be available within the necessary time interval?

570. The anticipated business volume?

571. Performance to date and material commitment?

572. Firewall Knowledge projected economic escalation?

573. Is accountability placed at the lowest-possible level within the Firewall Knowledge project so that decisions can be made at that level?

574. What are the assigned resources?

575. Will too many Signing-off responsibilities delay the completion of the activity/deliverable?

576. Where does all this information come from?

577. How many people do you need?

578. Are management actions taken to reduce indirect costs when there are significant adverse variances?

579. Time-phased control account budgets?

580. Do others have the time to dedicate to your Firewall Knowledge project?

581. Which resource planning tool provides information on resource responsibility and accountability?

582. Are the requirements for all items of overhead established by rational, traceable processes?

583. Undistributed budgets, if any?

2.28 Roles and Responsibilities: Firewall Knowledge

584. Once the responsibilities are defined for the Firewall Knowledge project, have the deliverables, roles and responsibilities been clearly communicated to every participant?

585. Be specific; avoid generalities. Thank you and great work alone are insufficient. What exactly do you appreciate and why?

586. Is the data complete?

587. Does the team have access to and ability to use data analysis tools?

588. Who is involved?

589. Concern: where are you limited or have no authority, where you can not influence?

590. How is your work-life balance?

591. Are governance roles and responsibilities documented?

592. Where are you most strong as a supervisor?

593. What is working well within your organizations performance management system?

594. What expectations were met?

595. What areas would you highlight for changes or improvements?

596. What should you do now to prepare yourself for a promotion, increased responsibilities or a different job?

597. Influence: what areas of organizational decision making are you able to influence when you do not have authority to make the final decision?

598. Are Firewall Knowledge project team roles and responsibilities identified and documented?

599. Is feedback clearly communicated and non-judgmental?

600. Do the values and practices inherent in the culture of your organization foster or hinder the process?

601. Attainable / achievable: the goal is attainable; can you actually accomplish the goal?

602. Once the responsibilities are defined for the Firewall Knowledge project, have the deliverables, roles and responsibilities been clearly communicated to every participant?

603. Are your policies supportive of a culture of quality data?

2.29 Human Resource Management Plan: Firewall Knowledge

604. Are the quality tools and methods identified in the Quality Plan appropriate to the Firewall Knowledge project?

605. Is there a formal set of procedures supporting Issues Management?

606. Does all Firewall Knowledge project documentation reside in a common repository for easy access?

607. How are you going to ensure that you have a well motivated workforce?

608. Are all payments made according to the contract(s)?

609. List roles. what commitments have been made?

610. Firewall Knowledge project definition & scope?

611. Do Firewall Knowledge project teams & team members report on status / activities / progress?

612. Who will be impacted (both positively and negatively) as a result of or during the execution of this Firewall Knowledge project?

613. Does the Firewall Knowledge project have a formal Firewall Knowledge project Charter?

614. Are target dates established for each milestone deliverable?

615. What skills, knowledge and experiences are required?

616. Has a resource management plan been created?

617. Is this Firewall Knowledge project carried out in partnership with other groups/organizations?

618. Responsiveness to change and the resulting demands for different skills and abilities?

619. Are the Firewall Knowledge project plans updated on a frequent basis?

2.30 Communications Management Plan: Firewall Knowledge

620. What communications method?

621. Who is involved as you identify stakeholders?

622. Are you constantly rushing from meeting to meeting?

623. Who is the stakeholder?

624. Are there common objectives between the team and the stakeholder?

625. How will the person responsible for executing the communication item be notified?

626. Which stakeholders are thought leaders, influences, or early adopters?

627. Do you feel more overwhelmed by stakeholders?

628. Are there too many who have an interest in some aspect of your work?

629. What approaches do you use?

630. What does the stakeholder need from the team?

631. What approaches to you feel are the best ones to use?

632. Do you feel a register helps?

633. Which stakeholders can influence others?

634. Why is stakeholder engagement important?

635. How often do you engage with stakeholders?

636. Are there potential barriers between the team and the stakeholder?

637. Can you think of other people who might have concerns or interests?

638. Who is responsible?

639. How is this initiative related to other portfolios, programs, or Firewall Knowledge projects?

2.31 Risk Management Plan: Firewall Knowledge

640. Do end-users have realistic expectations?

641. Was an original risk assessment/risk management plan completed?

642. What should be done with non-critical risks?

643. What will the damage be?

644. Are Firewall Knowledge project requirements stable?

645. Has something like this been done before?

646. Is there additional information that would make you more confident about your analysis?

647. What would you do?

648. What is the probability the risk avoidance strategy will be successful?

649. Is the process supported by tools?

650. Is Firewall Knowledge project scope stable?

651. Should the risk be taken at all?

652. Does the Firewall Knowledge project have the authority and ability to avoid the risk?

653. Degree of confidence in estimated size estimate?

654. How is the audit profession changing?

655. How would you suggest monitoring for risk transition indicators?

656. Where are you confronted with risks during the business phases?

657. Risk probability and impact: how will the probabilities and impacts of risk items be assessed?

2.32 Risk Register: Firewall Knowledge

658. How often will the Risk Management Plan and Risk Register be formally reviewed, and by whom?

659. Who needs to know about this?

660. What are the assumptions and current status that support the assessment of the risk?

661. Schedule impact/severity estimated range (workdays) assume the event happens, what is the potential impact?

662. How is a Community Risk Register created?

663. What has changed since the last period?

664. Manageability – have mitigations to the risk been identified?

665. What are your key risks/show istoppers and what is being done to manage them?

666. What may happen or not go according to plan?

667. What are you going to do to limit the Firewall Knowledge projects risk exposure due to the identified risks?

668. Why would you develop a risk register?

669. Preventative actions - planned actions to reduce the likelihood a risk will occur and/or reduce the seriousness should it occur. What should you do now?

670. When will it happen?

671. Are implemented controls working as others should?

672. Financial risk -can your organization afford to undertake the Firewall Knowledge project?

673. Who is going to do it?

674. Have other controls and solutions been implemented in other services which could be applied as an alternative to additional funding?

675. Are there any gaps in the evidence?

676. What is a Community Risk Register?

677. What should you do now?

2.33 Probability and Impact Assessment: Firewall Knowledge

678. What will be the likely political situation during the life of the Firewall Knowledge project?

679. What is the past performance of the Firewall Knowledge project manager?

680. What is the probability of the risk occurring?

681. Do the people have the right combinations of skills?

682. What are the preparations required for facing difficulties?

683. What things are likely to change?

684. Does the customer have a solid idea of what is required?

685. Are tools for analysis and design available?

686. What are its business ethics?

687. Do requirements put excessive performance constraints on the product?

688. Are tool mentors available?

689. What are the chances the event will occur?

690. Risk urgency assessment -which of your risks could occur soon, or require a longer planning time?

691. Your customers business requirements have suddenly shifted because of a new regulatory statute, what now?

692. Who has experience with this?

693. Is security a central objective?

694. When and how will the recent breakthroughs in basic research lead to commercial products?

695. Who should be notified of the occurrence of each of the risk indicators?

696. Are flexibility and reuse paramount?

697. What risks are necessary to achieve success?

2.34 Probability and Impact Matrix: Firewall Knowledge

698. How do risks change during the Firewall Knowledge projects life cycle?

699. Have staff received necessary training?

700. Premium on reliability of product?

701. Are the best people available?

702. Pay attention to the quality of the plans: is the content complete, or does it seem to be lacking detail?

703. What would you do differently?

704. What are the levels of understanding of the future users of this technology?

705. Can you stabilize dynamic risk factors?

706. How would you assess the risk management process in the Firewall Knowledge project?

707. What should be done NEXT?

708. During Firewall Knowledge project executing, a major problem occurs that was not included in the risk register. What should you do FIRST?

709. How much risk do others need to take?

710. What are the uncertainties associated with the technology selected for the Firewall Knowledge project?

711. During Firewall Knowledge project executing, a team member identifies a risk that is not in the risk register. What should you do?

712. What kind of preparation would be required to do this?

713. Have customers been involved fully in the definition of requirements?

714. Which of the risk factors can be avoided altogether?

2.35 Risk Data Sheet: Firewall Knowledge

715. What do you know?

716. What is the duration of infection (the length of time the host is infected with the organizm) in a normal healthy human host?

717. How do you handle product safely?

718. What are you weak at and therefore need to do better?

719. What can happen?

720. Potential for recurrence?

721. What actions can be taken to eliminate or remove risk?

722. What is the environment within which you operate (social trends, economic, community values, broad based participation, national directions etc.)?

723. What were the Causes that contributed?

724. Will revised controls lead to tolerable risk levels?

725. What are the main opportunities available to you that you should grab while you can?

726. What can you do?

727. Whom do you serve (customers)?

728. Are new hazards created?

729. Do effective diagnostic tests exist?

730. If it happens, what are the consequences?

731. Has the most cost-effective solution been chosen?

732. What do people affected think about the need for, and practicality of preventive measures?

733. How can hazards be reduced?

734. What are you trying to achieve (Objectives)?

2.36 Procurement Management Plan: Firewall Knowledge

735. Is there a procurement management plan in place?

736. Does the Firewall Knowledge project team have the right skills?

737. Is quality monitored from the perspective of the customers needs and expectations?

738. Why do you do it?

739. Is a payment system in place with proper reviews and approvals?

740. What communication items need improvement?

741. Is Firewall Knowledge project work proceeding in accordance with the original Firewall Knowledge project schedule?

742. Is there a Quality Management Plan?

743. Are the quality tools and methods identified in the Quality Plan appropriate to the Firewall Knowledge project?

744. Does the resource management plan include a personnel development plan?

745. If standardized procurement documents are

needed, where can others be found?

746. Have adequate resources been provided by management to ensure Firewall Knowledge project success?

747. Do you have the reasons why the changes to your organizational systems and capabilities are required?

748. Was the Firewall Knowledge project schedule reviewed by all stakeholders and formally accepted?

749. In which phase of the Acquisition Process Cycle does source qualifications reside?

750. Is it possible to track all classes of Firewall Knowledge project work (e.g. scheduled, un-scheduled, defect repair, etc.)?

2.37 Source Selection Criteria: Firewall Knowledge

751. Do you prepare an independent cost estimate?

752. How will you decide an evaluators write up is sufficient?

753. Do you want to have them collaborate at subfactor level?

754. How should the preproposal conference be conducted?

755. How and when do you enter into Firewall Knowledge project Procurement Management?

756. What information may not be provided?

757. How do you facilitate evaluation against published criteria?

758. What past performance information should be requested?

759. What is the basis of an estimate and what assumptions were made?

760. What benefits are accrued from issuing a DRFP in advance of issuing a final RFP?

761. What are the most critical evaluation criteria that prove to be tiebreakers in the evaluation of proposals?

762. When is it appropriate to conduct a preproposal conference?

763. What aspects should the contracting officer brief the Firewall Knowledge project on prior to evaluation of proposals?

764. Are there any specific considerations that precludes offers from being selected as the awardee?

765. How should the oral presentations be handled?

766. How much past performance information should be requested?

767. If the costs are normalized, please account for how the normalization is conducted. Is a cost realism analysis used?

768. Can you prevent comparison of proposals?

769. How organization are proposed quotes/prices?

770. How is past performance evaluated?

2.38 Stakeholder Management Plan: Firewall Knowledge

771. Are there any potential occupational health and safety issues due to the proposed purchases?

772. What training requirements are there based upon the required skills and resources?

773. Is there a formal set of procedures supporting Stakeholder Management?

774. Is it possible to track all classes of Firewall Knowledge project work (e.g. scheduled, unscheduled, defect repair, etc.)?

775. Were the budget estimates reasonable?

776. Is there an onboarding process in place?

777. What is to be the method of release?

778. Are schedule deliverables actually delivered?

779. How, to whom and how frequently will Risk status be reported?

780. Are the results of quality assurance reviews provided to affected groups & individuals?

781. Is the amount of effort justified by the anticipated value of forming a new process?

782. Does the Firewall Knowledge project have a formal Firewall Knowledge project Charter?

783. How is information analyzed, and what specific pieces of data would be of interest to the Firewall Knowledge project manager?

784. Is the communication plan being followed?

785. What is the general purpose in defining responsibilities of the already stated affiliated with the Firewall Knowledge project?

786. Are stakeholders aware and supportive of the principles and practices of modern software estimation?

787. Who will perform the review(s)?

788. Are Firewall Knowledge project contact logs kept up to date?

789. What are the procedures and processes to be followed for purchases, including approval and authorisation requirements?

790. Are vendor contract reports, reviews and visits conducted periodically?

2.39 Change Management Plan: Firewall Knowledge

791. Clearly articulate the overall business benefits of the Firewall Knowledge project -why are you doing this now?

792. How frequently should you repeat the message?

793. What does a resilient organization look like?

794. Who will do the training?

795. Has an information & communications plan been developed?

796. What is the worst thing that can happen if you communicate information?

797. Is it the same for each of the business units?

798. Different application of an existing process?

799. Which relationships will change?

800. Will a different work structure focus people on what is important?

801. Will the readiness criteria be met prior to the training roll out?

802. How will the stakeholders share information and transfer knowledge?

803. How does the principle of senders and receivers make the Firewall Knowledge project communications effort more complex?

804. Will all field readiness criteria have been practically met prior to training roll-out?

805. What can you do to minimise misinterpretation and negative perceptions?

806. Who might be able to help you the most?

807. When developing your communication plan do you address : When should the given message be communicated?

808. Has the priority for this Firewall Knowledge project been set by the Business Unit Management Team?

809. What prerequisite knowledge or training is required?

810. What will be the preferred method of delivery?

3.0 Executing Process Group: Firewall Knowledge

811. Will additional funds be needed for hardware or software?

812. How is Firewall Knowledge project performance information created and distributed?

813. What are the typical Firewall Knowledge project management skills?

814. How well did the chosen processes produce the expected results?

815. What does it mean to take a systems view of a Firewall Knowledge project?

816. Do the partners have sufficient financial capacity to keep up the benefits produced by the programme?

817. Mitigate. what will you do to minimize the impact should a risk event occur?

818. Would you rate yourself as being risk-averse, risk-neutral, or risk-seeking?

819. How can software assist in Firewall Knowledge project communications?

820. How many different communication channels does the Firewall Knowledge project team have?

821. What is in place for ensuring adequate change control on Firewall Knowledge projects that involve outside contracts?

822. In what way has the program come up with innovative measures for problem-solving?

823. What business situation is being addressed?

824. What good practices or successful experiences or transferable examples have been identified?

825. Are escalated issues resolved promptly?

826. How could you control progress of your Firewall Knowledge project?

827. What are the main types of contracts if you do decide to outsource?

828. What are crucial elements of successful Firewall Knowledge project plan execution?

829. How well did the chosen processes fit the needs of the Firewall Knowledge project?

830. How does a Firewall Knowledge project life cycle differ from a product life cycle?

3.1 Team Member Status Report: Firewall Knowledge

831. How it is to be done?

832. Does every department have to have a Firewall Knowledge project Manager on staff?

833. How will resource planning be done?

834. Are the products of your organizations Firewall Knowledge projects meeting customers objectives?

835. How much risk is involved?

836. Are the attitudes of staff regarding Firewall Knowledge project work improving?

837. How does this product, good, or service meet the needs of the Firewall Knowledge project and your organization as a whole?

838. What is to be done?

839. Why is it to be done?

840. What specific interest groups do you have in place?

841. Do you have an Enterprise Firewall Knowledge project Management Office (EPMO)?

842. How can you make it practical?

843. The problem with Reward & Recognition Programs is that the truly deserving people all too often get left out. How can you make it practical?

844. Will the staff do training or is that done by a third party?

845. When a teams productivity and success depend on collaboration and the efficient flow of information, what generally fails them?

846. Is there evidence that staff is taking a more professional approach toward management of your organizations Firewall Knowledge projects?

847. Are your organizations Firewall Knowledge projects more successful over time?

848. Does your organization have the means (staff, money, contract, etc.) to produce or to acquire the product, good, or service?

849. Does the product, good, or service already exist within your organization?

3.2 Change Request: Firewall Knowledge

850. Are there requirements attributes that are strongly related to the complexity and size?

851. Why control change across the life cycle?

852. Are change requests logged and managed?

853. Will this change conflict with other requirements changes (e.g., lead to conflicting operational scenarios)?

854. What type of changes does change control take into account?

855. What should be regulated in a change control operating instruction?

856. Has your address changed?

857. How can changes be graded?

858. What needs to be communicated?

859. Who needs to approve change requests?

860. Will all change requests be unconditionally tracked through this process?

861. Who is included in the change control team?

862. When do you create a change request?

863. How do team members communicate with each other?

864. What are the Impacts to your organization?

865. Where do changes come from?

866. Have all related configuration items been properly updated?

867. How well do experienced software developers predict software change?

868. Since there are no change requests in your Firewall Knowledge project at this point, what must you have before you begin?

869. What must be taken into consideration when introducing change control programs?

3.3 Change Log: Firewall Knowledge

870. When was the request submitted?

871. Is this a mandatory replacement?

872. How does this change affect the timeline of the schedule?

873. Is the change request open, closed or pending?

874. Should a more thorough impact analysis be conducted?

875. Who initiated the change request?

876. Is the submitted change a new change or a modification of a previously approved change?

877. When was the request approved?

878. Will the Firewall Knowledge project fail if the change request is not executed?

879. Is the requested change request a result of changes in other Firewall Knowledge project(s)?

880. Do the described changes impact on the integrity or security of the system?

881. Does the suggested change request represent a desired enhancement to the products functionality?

882. How does this change affect scope?

883. Is the change backward compatible without limitations?

884. How does this relate to the standards developed for specific business processes?

885. Is the change request within Firewall Knowledge project scope?

886. Does the suggested change request seem to represent a necessary enhancement to the product?

3.4 Decision Log: Firewall Knowledge

887. What is your overall strategy for quality control / quality assurance procedures?

888. Does anything need to be adjusted?

889. How do you know when you are achieving it?

890. With whom was the decision shared or considered?

891. How consolidated and comprehensive a story can you tell by capturing currently available incident data in a central location and through a log of key decisions during an incident?

892. Behaviors; what are guidelines that the team has identified that will assist them with getting the most out of team meetings?

893. How effective is maintaining the log at facilitating organizational learning?

894. What eDiscovery problem or issue did your organization set out to fix or make better?

895. How does provision of information, both in terms of content and presentation, influence acceptance of alternative strategies?

896. Decision-making process; how will the team make decisions?

897. Adversarial environment. is your opponent open to a non-traditional workflow, or will it likely challenge anything you do?

898. Is your opponent open to a non-traditional workflow, or will it likely challenge anything you do?

899. What is the line where eDiscovery ends and document review begins?

900. What was the rationale for the decision?

901. How do you define success?

902. Do strategies and tactics aimed at less than full control reduce the costs of management or simply shift the cost burden?

903. How does an increasing emphasis on cost containment influence the strategies and tactics used?

904. What is the average size of your matters in an applicable measurement?

905. Linked to original objective?

906. Which variables make a critical difference?

3.5 Quality Audit: Firewall Knowledge

907. Are all complaints involving the possible failure of a device, labeling, or packaging to meet any of its specifications reviewed, evaluated, and investigated?

908. How does your organization know that its system for attending to the particular needs of its international staff is appropriately effective and constructive?

909. How does your organization know that its system for ensuring that its training activities are appropriately resourced and support is appropriately effective and constructive?

910. How does your organization know that its support services planning and management systems are appropriately effective and constructive?

911. How does your organization know that its teaching activities (and staff learning) are effectively and constructively enhanced by its activities?

912. Does your organization have set of goals, objectives, strategies and targets that are clearly understood by the Board and staff?

913. What are the main things that hinder your ability to do a good job?

914. Is your organizations resource allocation system properly aligned with its collection of intentions?

915. What does an analysis of your organizations staff profile suggest in terms of its planning, and how is this being addressed?

916. What does the organizarion look for in a Quality audit?

917. How does your organization know that its research funding systems are appropriately effective and constructive in enabling quality research outcomes?

918. Is your organizational structure a help or a hindrance to deployment?

919. How does your organization know that its systems for meeting staff extracurricular learning support requirements are appropriately effective and constructive?

920. How does your organization know that the quality of its supervisors is appropriately effective and constructive?

921. How does your organization know that its relationships with industry and employers are appropriately effective and constructive?

922. Are measuring and test equipment that have been placed out of service suitably identified and excluded from use in any device reconditioning operation?

923. How does your organization know that its relationships with the community at large are appropriately effective and constructive?

924. How does your organization know that its Mission, Vision and Values Statements are appropriate and effectively guiding your organization?

925. How does your organization ensure that equipment is appropriately maintained and producing valid results?

926. Do the suppliers use a formal quality system?

3.6 Team Directory: Firewall Knowledge

927. Who will be the stakeholders on your next Firewall Knowledge project?

928. Who is the Sponsor?

929. Where will the product be used and/or delivered or built when appropriate?

930. Who are your stakeholders (customers, sponsors, end users, team members)?

931. Decisions: what could be done better to improve the quality of the constructed product?

932. Contract requirements complied with?

933. What are you going to deliver or accomplish?

934. Process decisions: do invoice amounts match accepted work in place?

935. Have you decided when to celebrate the Firewall Knowledge projects completion date?

936. Decisions: is the most suitable form of contract being used?

937. Process decisions: which organizational elements and which individuals will be assigned management functions?

938. When will you produce deliverables?

939. Process decisions: how well was task order work performed?

940. Who should receive information (all stakeholders)?

941. Is construction on schedule?

942. Process decisions: are all start-up, turn over and close out requirements of the contract satisfied?

943. Days from the time the issue is identified?

944. Who will write the meeting minutes and distribute?

945. Why is the work necessary?

3.7 Team Operating Agreement: Firewall Knowledge

946. What resources can be provided for the team in terms of equipment, space, time for training, protected time and space for meetings, and travel allowances?

947. What is culture?

948. Did you prepare participants for the next meeting?

949. What is a Virtual Team?

950. Seconds for members to respond?

951. Does your team need access to all documents and information at all times?

952. Resource allocation: how will individual team members account for time and expenses, and how will this be allocated in the team budget?

953. Do you upload presentation materials in advance and test the technology?

954. Are there the right people on your team?

955. How will you divide work equitably?

956. Do you brief absent members after they view meeting notes or listen to a recording?

957. Are leadership responsibilities shared among team members (versus a single leader)?

958. Has the appropriate access to relevant data and analysis capability been granted?

959. What are the safety issues/risks that need to be addressed and/or that the team needs to consider?

960. What is the anticipated procedure (recruitment, solicitation of volunteers, or assignment) for selecting team members?

961. What types of accommodations will be formulated and put in place for sustaining the team?

962. Do you record meetings for the already stated unable to attend?

963. Confidentiality: how will confidential information be handled?

964. Do team members reside in more than two countries?

965. Have you set the goals and objectives of the team?

3.8 Team Performance Assessment: Firewall Knowledge

966. Can familiarity breed backup?

967. To what degree are the teams goals and objectives clear, simple, and measurable?

968. Do you give group members authority to make at least some important decisions?

969. To what degree does the teams work approach provide opportunity for members to engage in open interaction?

970. Where to from here?

971. What do you think is the most constructive thing that could be done now to resolve considerations and disputes about method variance?

972. How does Firewall Knowledge project termination impact Firewall Knowledge project team members?

973. To what degree is the team cognizant of small wins to be celebrated along the way?

974. To what degree can team members frequently and easily communicate with one another?

975. Delaying market entry: how long is too long?

976. To what degree can team members vigorously define the teams purpose in considerations with others who are not part of the functioning team?

977. If you are worried about method variance before you collect data, what sort of design elements might you include to reduce or eliminate the threat of method variance?

978. To what degree will the team adopt a concrete, clearly understood, and agreed-upon approach that will result in achievement of the teams goals?

979. To what degree can all members engage in open and interactive considerations?

980. To what degree do members understand and articulate the same purpose without relying on ambiguous abstractions?

981. Do friends perform better than acquaintances?

982. How much interpersonal friction is there in your team?

983. To what degree are sub-teams possible or necessary?

984. To what degree are corresponding categories of skills either actually or potentially represented across the membership?

985. To what degree do team members feel that the purpose of the team is important, if not exciting?

3.9 Team Member Performance Assessment: Firewall Knowledge

986. How is your organizations Strategic Management System tied to performance measurement?

987. How often are assessments to be conducted?

988. Who they are?

989. What qualities does a successful Team leader possess?

990. What steps have you taken to improve performance?

991. How should adaptive assessments be implemented?

992. What is used as a basis for instructional decisions?

993. New skills/knowledge gained this year?

994. To what degree can team members meet frequently enough to accomplish the teams ends?

995. What variables that affect team members achievement are within your control?

996. What evidence supports your decision-making?

997. Is it critical or vital to the job?

998. How are training activities developed from a technical perspective?

999. Verify business objectives. Are they appropriate, and well-articulated?

1000. Did training work?

1001. What are they responsible for?

1002. How do you make use of research?

1003. To what degree are the goals ambitious?

1004. Where can team members go for more detailed information on performance measurement and assessment?

3.10 Issue Log: Firewall Knowledge

1005. How is this initiative related to other portfolios, programs, or Firewall Knowledge projects?

1006. What is the stakeholders political influence?

1007. Is there an important stakeholder who is actively opposed and will not receive messages?

1008. Why do you manage communications?

1009. What is a change?

1010. Who is the issue assigned to?

1011. What is the status of the issue?

1012. What are the stakeholders interrelationships?

1013. How were past initiatives successful?

1014. Who needs to know and how much?

1015. What would have to change?

1016. Is the issue log kept in a safe place?

1017. How do you reply to this question; you am new here and managing this major program. How do you suggest you build your network?

4.0 Monitoring and Controlling Process Group: Firewall Knowledge

1018. Based on your Firewall Knowledge project communication management plan, what worked well?

1019. Is the program making progress in helping to achieve the set results?

1020. What areas were overlooked on this Firewall Knowledge project?

1021. What is the expected monetary value of the Firewall Knowledge project?

1022. How were collaborations developed, and how are they sustained?

1023. Are the necessary foundations in place to ensure the sustainability of the results of the programme?

1024. How well did the chosen processes fit the needs of the Firewall Knowledge project?

1025. Overall, how does the program function to serve the clients?

1026. How can you monitor progress?

1027. What resources are necessary?

1028. Is the program in place as intended?

1029. How is agile program management done?

1030. If action is called for, what form should it take?

1031. Who needs to be engaged upfront to ensure use of results?

4.1 Project Performance Report: Firewall Knowledge

1032. What is the PRS?

1033. Next Steps?

1034. How is the data used?

1035. To what degree will the approach capitalize on and enhance the skills of all team members in a manner that takes into consideration other demands on members of the team?

1036. What is in it for you?

1037. To what degree does the funding match the requirement?

1038. To what degree does the teams purpose contain themes that are particularly meaningful and memorable?

1039. To what degree do individual skills and abilities match task demands?

1040. To what degree can the team measure progress against specific goals?

1041. To what degree is the information network consistent with the structure of the formal organization?

1042. To what degree are the demands of the task compatible with and converge with the relationships of the informal organization?

1043. To what degree does the teams work approach provide opportunity for members to engage in results-based evaluation?

1044. To what degree will the team ensure that all members equitably share the work essential to the success of the team?

1045. To what degree are the goals realistic?

1046. To what degree will team members, individually and collectively, commit time to help themselves and others learn and develop skills?

1047. To what degree are the demands of the task compatible with and converge with the mission and functions of the formal organization?

1048. To what degree can the cognitive capacity of individuals accommodate the flow of information?

4.2 Variance Analysis: Firewall Knowledge

1049. What is the expected future profitability of each customer?

1050. When, during the last four quarters, did a primary business event occur causing a fluctuation?

1051. How are material, labor, and overhead standards set?

1052. What is the budgeted cost for work scheduled?

1053. What types of services and expense are shared between business segments?

1054. Are the overhead pools formally and adequately identified?

1055. Did a new competitor enter the market?

1056. Are records maintained to show how undistributed budgets are controlled?

1057. Can the contractor substantiate work package and planning package budgets?

1058. Are there externalities from having some customers, even if they are unprofitable in the short run?

1059. Contemplated overhead expenditure for each

period based on the best information currently is available?

1060. Who is generally responsible for monitoring and taking action on variances?

1061. Are there changes in the direct base to which overhead costs are allocated?

1062. How are variances affected by multiple material and labor categories?

1063. Do work packages consist of discrete tasks which are adequately described?

1064. How does the monthly budget compare to the actual experience?

1065. Is the anticipated (firm and potential) business base Firewall Knowledge projected in a rational, consistent manner?

1066. Are estimates of costs at completion generated in a rational, consistent manner?

1067. How does your organization measure performance?

4.3 Earned Value Status: Firewall Knowledge

1068. How much is it going to cost by the finish?

1069. When is it going to finish?

1070. Earned value can be used in almost any Firewall Knowledge project situation and in almost any Firewall Knowledge project environment. it may be used on large Firewall Knowledge projects, medium sized Firewall Knowledge projects, tiny Firewall Knowledge projects (in cut-down form), complex and simple Firewall Knowledge projects and in any market sector. some people, of course, know all about earned value, they have used it for years - but perhaps not as effectively as they could have?

1071. Where is evidence-based earned value in your organization reported?

1072. Verification is a process of ensuring that the developed system satisfies the stakeholders agreements and specifications; Are you building the product right? What do you haverify?

1073. If earned value management (EVM) is so good in determining the true status of a Firewall Knowledge project and Firewall Knowledge project its completion, why is it that hardly any one uses it in information systems related Firewall Knowledge projects?

1074. Where are your problem areas?

1075. Are you hitting your Firewall Knowledge projects targets?

1076. Validation is a process of ensuring that the developed system will actually achieve the stakeholders desired outcomes; Are you building the right product? What do you validate?

1077. How does this compare with other Firewall Knowledge projects?

1078. What is the unit of forecast value?

4.4 Risk Audit: Firewall Knowledge

1079. Have you considered the health and safety of everyone in your organization and do you meet work health and safety regulations?

1080. Are contracts reviewed before renewal?

1081. Strategic business risk audit methodologies; are corresponding an attempt to sell other services, and is management becoming the client of the audit rather than the shareholder?

1082. Is the customer technically sophisticated in the product area?

1083. Is your organization able to present documentary evidence in support of compliance?

1084. Do you have a consistent repeatable process that is actually used?

1085. What expertise does the Board have on quality, outcomes, and errors?

1086. Do you have an understanding of insurance claims processes?

1087. What is the implication of budget constraint on this process?

1088. Can assurance be expanded beyond the traditional audit without undermining independence?

1089. Is all required equipment available?

1090. Are you aware of the industry standards that apply to your operations?

1091. Management -what contingency plans do you have if the risk becomes a reality?

1092. What resources are needed to achieve program results?

1093. What are the benefits of a Enterprise wide approach to Risk Management?

1094. Are policies communicated to all affected?

1095. Have reasonable steps been taken to reduce the risks to acceptable levels?

1096. Do you conduct risk assessments on all programs, activities and events?

1097. Are you willing to seek legal advice when required?

4.5 Contractor Status Report: Firewall Knowledge

1098. Are there contractual transfer concerns?

1099. What was the overall budget or estimated cost?

1100. Describe how often regular updates are made to the proposed solution. Are corresponding regular updates included in the standard maintenance plan?

1101. What was the budget or estimated cost for your organizations services?

1102. If applicable; describe your standard schedule for new software version releases. Are new software version releases included in the standard maintenance plan?

1103. What process manages the contracts?

1104. Who can list a Firewall Knowledge project as organization experience, your organization or a previous employee of your organization?

1105. What are the minimum and optimal bandwidth requirements for the proposed soluiton?

1106. What was the actual budget or estimated cost for your organizations services?

1107. How does the proposed individual meet each requirement?

1108. What is the average response time for answering a support call?

1109. What was the final actual cost?

1110. How is risk transferred?

1111. How long have you been using the services?

4.6 Formal Acceptance: Firewall Knowledge

1112. What can you do better next time?

1113. Did the Firewall Knowledge project achieve its MOV?

1114. How does your team plan to obtain formal acceptance on your Firewall Knowledge project?

1115. What function(s) does it fill or meet?

1116. Is formal acceptance of the Firewall Knowledge project product documented and distributed?

1117. What lessons were learned about your Firewall Knowledge project management methodology?

1118. Who supplies data?

1119. What is the Acceptance Management Process?

1120. How well did the team follow the methodology?

1121. Was business value realized?

1122. Was the Firewall Knowledge project goal achieved?

1123. General estimate of the costs and times to complete the Firewall Knowledge project?

1124. Was the sponsor/customer satisfied?

1125. Have all comments been addressed?

1126. Do you buy-in installation services?

1127. Was the Firewall Knowledge project managed well?

1128. What features, practices, and processes proved to be strengths or weaknesses?

1129. Did the Firewall Knowledge project manager and team act in a professional and ethical manner?

1130. Does it do what client said it would?

1131. Do you perform formal acceptance or burn-in tests?

5.0 Closing Process Group: Firewall Knowledge

1132. What is an Encumbrance?

1133. Did you do things well?

1134. Will the Firewall Knowledge project deliverable(s) replace a current asset or group of assets?

1135. Can the lesson learned be replicated?

1136. Specific - is the objective clear in terms of what, how, when, and where the situation will be changed?

1137. What were the desired outcomes?

1138. Who are the Firewall Knowledge project stakeholders?

1139. What were the actual outcomes?

1140. Did the Firewall Knowledge project management methodology work?

1141. Did you do what you said you were going to do?

1142. What will you do?

1143. What areas were overlooked on this Firewall Knowledge project?

1144. Are there funding or time constraints?

1145. What was learned?

5.1 Procurement Audit: Firewall Knowledge

1146. Are the official minutes written in a clear and concise manner?

1147. Is the weighting set coherent, convincing and leaving little scope for arbitrary and random evaluation and ranking?

1148. Were all admitted tenderers invited to submit a tender for each specific contract?

1149. When you set social or environmental conditions for the performance of the contract, were corresponding compatible with the law and was adequate information given to the candidates?

1150. Relevance of the contract to the Internal Market?

1151. Are checks used in numeric sequence?

1152. Are there policies regarding special approval for capital expenditures?

1153. Is there a general policy on approval of purchases?

1154. Are there performance targets on value for money obtained and cost savings?

1155. Are all complaints of late or incorrect payment

sent to a person independent of the already stated having cash disbursement responsibilities?

1156. Are periodic audits made of disbursement activities?

1157. Is the foreseen budget compared with similar Firewall Knowledge projects or procurements yet realised (historical standards)?

1158. Is there no evidence that the expert has influenced the decisions taken by the public authority in his/her interest or in the interest of a specific contractor?

1159. Was the dynamic purchasing system set up following the rules of open procedure?

1160. Do your organizations policies promote and/or safeguard fair competition?

1161. How are you making the audit trail easy to follow?

1162. Is the departments procurement function/unit well organized?

1163. Were all interested operators allowed the opportunity to participate?

1164. Are incentives to deliver on time and in quantity properly specified?

1165. How do you monitor behaviour of procurement staff?

5.2 Contract Close-Out: Firewall Knowledge

1166. Have all contract records been included in the Firewall Knowledge project archives?

1167. Parties: Authorized?

1168. How is the contracting office notified of the automatic contract close-out?

1169. Are the signers the authorized officials?

1170. Have all contracts been closed?

1171. What happens to the recipient of services?

1172. Was the contract complete without requiring numerous changes and revisions?

1173. Change in circumstances?

1174. Parties: who is involved?

1175. Was the contract sufficiently clear so as not to result in numerous disputes and misunderstandings?

1176. What is capture management?

1177. Has each contract been audited to verify acceptance and delivery?

1178. Change in knowledge?

1179. How does it work?

1180. Have all contracts been completed?

1181. Have all acceptance criteria been met prior to final payment to contractors?

1182. Was the contract type appropriate?

1183. How/when used ?

1184. Change in attitude or behavior?

5.3 Project or Phase Close-Out: Firewall Knowledge

1185. Who controlled key decisions that were made?

1186. Is the lesson significant, valid, and applicable?

1187. Was the schedule met?

1188. What are the informational communication needs for each stakeholder?

1189. Is the lesson based on actual Firewall Knowledge project experience rather than on independent research?

1190. What process was planned for managing issues/risks?

1191. What advantages do the an individual interview have over a group meeting, and vice-versa?

1192. What are the marketing communication needs for each stakeholder?

1193. Were messages directly related to the release strategy or phases of the Firewall Knowledge project?

1194. Who controlled the resources for the Firewall Knowledge project?

1195. What stakeholder group needs, expectations, and interests are being met by the Firewall

Knowledge project?

1196. What was expected from each stakeholder?

1197. How often did each stakeholder need an update?

1198. Have business partners been involved extensively, and what data was required for them?

1199. What are they?

1200. Who are the Firewall Knowledge project stakeholders and what are roles and involvement?

1201. In preparing the Lessons Learned report, should it reflect a consensus viewpoint, or should the report reflect the different individual viewpoints?

1202. What hierarchical authority does the stakeholder have in your organization?

1203. Does the lesson describe a function that would be done differently the next time?

5.4 Lessons Learned: Firewall Knowledge

1204. Was sufficient time allocated to review Firewall Knowledge project deliverables?

1205. How well does the product or service the Firewall Knowledge project produced meet the defined Firewall Knowledge project requirements?

1206. Under what legal authority did your organization head and program manager direct your organization and Firewall Knowledge project?

1207. What was the geopolitical history during the origin of your organization and at the time of task input?

1208. What Firewall Knowledge project circumstances were not anticipated?

1209. Was there a Firewall Knowledge project Definition document. Was there a Firewall Knowledge project Plan. Were they used during the Firewall Knowledge project?

1210. What skills did you need that were missing on this Firewall Knowledge project?

1211. Is your organization willing to expose problems or mistakes for the betterment of the collective whole, and can you do this in a way that does not intimidate employees or workers?

1212. What was the single greatest success and the single greatest shortcoming or challenge from the Firewall Knowledge projects perspective?

1213. How effective was the training you received in preparation for the use of the product/service?

1214. Did the delivered product meet the specified requirements and goals of the Firewall Knowledge project?

1215. How complete and timely were the materials you were provided to decide whether to proceed from one Firewall Knowledge project lifecycle phase to the next?

1216. How efficient and effective were Firewall Knowledge project team meetings?

1217. How closely did deliverables match what was defined within the Firewall Knowledge project Scope?

1218. Were quality procedures built into the Firewall Knowledge project?

1219. If you had to do this Firewall Knowledge project again, what is the one thing that you would change (related to process, not to technical solutions)?

1220. What worked well or did not work well, either for this Firewall Knowledge project or for the Firewall Knowledge project team?

1221. Who had fiscal authority to manage the funding for the Firewall Knowledge project, did that work?

1222. How many government and contractor personnel are authorized for the Firewall Knowledge project?

1223. What is your overall assessment of the outcome of this Firewall Knowledge project?

Index

meetings   29-30, 36, 198, 205-206, 235
megatrends   83
member   5, 35, 92, 94, 142, 179, 192, 209
members   26, 32-33, 36, 75, 116, 123, 132, 168, 195, 203,
205-210, 214-215
membership   208
memorable   160, 214
mentors   176
message   188-189
messages   211, 232
method   112, 135, 152, 158, 170, 186, 189, 207-208
methods   33, 40, 125, 155, 159, 168, 182
metrics 4, 32, 39, 77, 105, 114-115, 160-161
milestone   3, 137, 139, 144, 169
milestones   36, 107, 115, 130, 140, 151
minimise   189
minimize   190
minimizing   53, 87
minimum   222
minority   18
minutes   35, 66, 204, 228
missed 47
missing 98, 136, 234
mission 50, 53, 83, 85, 202, 215
mistakes   234
Mitigate   190
mitigation   112, 115, 144, 150
modeling   49
models 21, 51, 84
modern   187
modified   62, 75
modifier   161
moment   80
moments   53
momentum   80
monetary   212
monitor   60, 69, 72, 74, 78, 108, 154, 212, 229
monitored   76, 134, 144, 146, 182
monitoring   5, 71, 74, 76, 78, 116, 141, 173, 212, 217
monthly   217
months 62, 66
motivate   95
motivated   168